What is this?

A flexible action pack of
teaching materials, activities and tools
to teach children about world mission
in a fun and non-threatening way.

Why do you need it?

World mission is often neglected in Sunday school and other youth teaching materials. Despite its presence from Genesis to Revelation, it is sometimes seen as a 'specialist' subject.

This pack supplements your normal teaching programme and is intended for:
- A 'Missions Sunday' at church
- A practical spot at summer camp
- Motivating your youth group to practical action
- Broadening the horizons of your school group

Who is it for?

Children: 7-11 years old
Groups: Sunday schools, youth groups, holiday clubs, summer camps, and families

Teachers: For teachers who want to focus on world mission but are not experts. This book provides enough background in each section to get you going. You'll enjoy it!
Events: This book will help you put together anything from a one-off filler or special event to a series of teaching sessions.

Copyright information

Station Approach, Borough Green, Sevenoaks, Kent, TN15 8BG, UK
www.omf.org.uk

Published by: **Christian Focus Publications**
Geanies House, Fearn, Tain, Ross-shire, IV20 1TW, Scotland
www.christianfocus.com

Illustrations by Tim Charnick
Cover design by Tim Charnick

ISBN 1 85792 4460

Pic'n'mix – The key to using this book

Pic'n'mix

There are no set lesson plans, nor one right way to teach these materials. They are flexible so that you can adapt them to the needs of your group.

You know your children better than anyone. You can choose a balance of teaching, activities and games that will help the children learn and grow, as well as enjoy themselves.

There are seven main sections to this book. These are easily identifiable by the black tabs:

- **Bible teaching**—what the Bible says about mission and telling others about Jesus
- **What's it like?**—what missionaries do
- **Kids like me**—what it would be like if you had been born in Asia
- **Support**—how to pray for missionaries and send them a parcel
- **Crafts and activities**—practical things to make or do related to missions and Asia
- **Games**—fun games to use up spare energy
- **Snacks and recipes**—tasty meals or nibbles to prepare before hand or make with the children

When putting together a programme, think about what lessons you want to teach in the time available. You may wish to start from the list of *Sample Lesson Plans* on pp 4-5. Some of these follow a theme (such as *prayer* or *evangelism*).

If you are focusing on a particular country, look at the *Index by country* on p 96.

Reproducible

You are free to make copies of this book for use in your class. We only ask that each person teaching the material purchase their own copy. See the copyright notice on p 1 for details.

How to make the best photocopies

When copying, you may not want the spine, page number or the black tabs to come out on the copies.

The easiest way to get rid of these is by sticking *Post-It* notes over the black tabs and page numbers.

These pages have also been designed so that you can set your photocopier to enlarge at 105%. This will take only the important teaching information, and will leave the rest.

You may also wish to browse the OMF web site [www.omf.org.uk/kids] where you can download these materials and print them directly from your computer.

Be enthusiastic!

There is no better way to kill off a subject than by making it dull, lifeless or irrelevant. Remember when you were at school. Which teachers made the most impact on you?

Look for help if you need it

No one is an expert in everything.

Make time to prepare the lessons before you teach them. Where you need help, don't be afraid to ask for it. Check out:

- Encyclopaedias, libraries, the web (OMF's address is www.omf.org.uk) for information on Asia, maps and flags
- People—talk to the missionaries from your church. Get up to date news from them and make it a feature of your lesson and your prayers together.

Pray

For each member of your group as an individual:

- For a deeper knowledge and love of God
- For a widening perspective on God's world
- For long term results

Key to symbols

Length of time:

10 minutes

15-20 minutes

30 minutes

These are rough guidelines.
Adapt each session to the needs of your group.

Contents

Sample lesson plans

Focus on China

Bible studies	Do I have to believe in Jesus to go to heaven?	p 10	10 mins
What's it like?	An English teacher in China	p 26	20 mins
Game	Lame chicken	p 83	10 mins
Craft	Chinese streamers	p 66	20 mins
Other ideas			**60 mins**
Kids like me	Wang Li Bing	p 46	10 mins
Snack	Chinese fried rice	p 88	30 mins
Craft	Write on!	p 73	5 mins

Focus on Japan

Bible studies	Why am I here?	p 8	10 mins
What's it like?	Bobby gets ready for a special job in Japan	p 28	15 mins
Craft	Japanese fan	p 68	15 mins
Game	Jan-Ken-Pon	p 85	5 mins
Other ideas			**45 mins**
Craft	Japanese song	p 76	5 mins
Kids like me	Hashimoto	p 44	10 mins
Game	Wakey, wakey!	p 78	10 mins

Focus on Evangelism

Bible studies	Why should I tell my friends about Jesus?	p 11	10 mins
What's it like?	A radio worker in Thailand	p 34	10 mins
Game	Mango, mango, durian!	p 82	10 mins
Game	The drinking game	p 85	5 mins
Other ideas			**35 mins**
What's it like?	A church worker in Thailand	p 36	10 mins
Snack	Mango ice-cream	p 90	20 mins

Focus on God's plan for my life

Bible studies	Why am I here?	p 8	10 mins
What's it like?	Bobby gets ready for a special job in Japan	p 28	15 mins
Craft	International face painting	p 66	30 mins
Game	Chop suey!	p 82	5 mins
Other ideas			**60 mins**
Game	The Great Crab Race	p 84	10 mins
Game	The Great Peanut Race	p 84	10 mins

Focus on Prayer

Bible studies	Do my prayers make a difference?	p 9	10 mins
What's it like?	An English teacher in China	p 26	15 mins
Craft	Gecko Mania 1	p 63	10 mins
Support	How to pray for Asian non-Christians	p 58	10 mins
Other ideas			**45 mins**
Craft	Gecko mania 2	p 63	20 mins
Game	Shoe scramble	p 79	10 mins

Focus on Bible translation

Bible studies	Do I have to believe in Jesus to go to heaven?	p 10	10 mins
What's it like?	To be a Bible translator in the Philippines 1	p 30	20 mins
Craft	Write on!	p 73	10 mins
Game	Munch, munch, you're lunch!	p 86	10 mins
Support	How to pray for Asian Christians	p 57	10 mins
Other ideas			**60 mins**
What's it like?	To be a Bible translator in the Philippines 2	p 32	20 mins
Craft	Japanese wordsearch	p 73	10 mins

Sample lesson plans

Focus on Support

Bible studies	Do my prayers make a difference?	p 9	10 mins
What's it like?	My first week in Asia 1	p 18	15 mins
Support	Send a care package	p 54	15 mins
Craft	Pop-up jungle snake	p 67	20 mins
Other ideas			**60 mins**
Game	At the market stall	p 81	10 mins
Game	The toilet game	p 79	5 mins
What's it like?	My first week in Asia 2	p 20	15 mins

Focus on Missionary Kids

Bible studies	Why am I here?	p 8	10 mins
What's it like?	To be a missionary kid 1	p 22	15 mins
Game	I packed my bag	p 78	10 mins
Craft	The jet set	p 72	10 mins
Other ideas			**45 mins**
Game	Fasten your seatbelts!	p 80	10 mins
Support	How to pray for missionary kids	p 56	10 mins
Kids like me	Onka-Shooey	p 50	10 mins

Studies in Jonah 1

Bible studies	The Great Escape	p 12	15 mins
What's it like?	Bobby gets ready for a special job in Japan	p 28	15 mins
Craft	Your passport, please!	p 60	10 mins
Game	I packed my bag	p 78	10 mins
Other ideas			**50 mins**
Game	Chop suey!	p 82	10 mins
Game	The toilet game	p 79	5 mins

Studies in Jonah 2

Bible studies	The Great Rescue	p 13	15 mins
What's it like?	To be a Bible translator in the Philippines 1	p 30	20 mins
Craft	Song in Tagalog	p 76	5 mins
Game	Munch, munch, you're lunch!	p 86	10 mins
Other ideas			**50 mins**
Snack	Coconut milk shake	p 89	15 mins
Game	The drinking game	p 85	5 mins

Studies in Jonah 3

Bible studies	The Great Turn	p 14	15 mins
What's it like?	To be a Bible translator in the Philippines 2	p 32	20 mins
Kids like me	Donnalyn	p 48	10 mins
Game	Presohan	p 83	10 mins
Other ideas			**55 mins**
Support	How to pray for Asian non-Christians	p 58	10 mins
Game	Wakey, wakey!	p 78	10 mins

Studies in Jonah 4

Bible studies	The Great Sulk	p 15	15 mins
What's it like?	To be a medical missionary 1	p 38	15 mins
Game	Dressing up	p 80	15 mins
Other ideas			**45 mins**
Snack	Fruit feast with coconut dip	p 89	20 mins
Kids like me	Wang Li Bing	p 46	10 mins
Craft	International face painting	p 66	45 mins

About OMF

A brief history of time

In 1865, the same year that slavery was abolished in America and Abraham Lincoln was killed by an assassin's bullet, **James Hudson Taylor** founded the China Inland Mission. A year later Hudson Taylor, 17 adults and four children, sail for China.

By 1950 the number of Chinese church members numbered over 700,000, but the coming to power of Mao Zedong made it impossible for missionaries to remain in China. So CIM (the China Inland Mission) sought to reach Chinese in parts of Asia still open to the gospel, and changed its name to CIM/OMF.

Today OMF is an international movement with 1,000 members from 30 nations reaching some 70 people groups in East Asia. Many who join OMF do so as 'career' missionaries, though many go out with us on a short-term basis. Others serve Christ by taking their professional skills to 'creative access nations' which are closed to missionaries, but welcome foreign expertise.

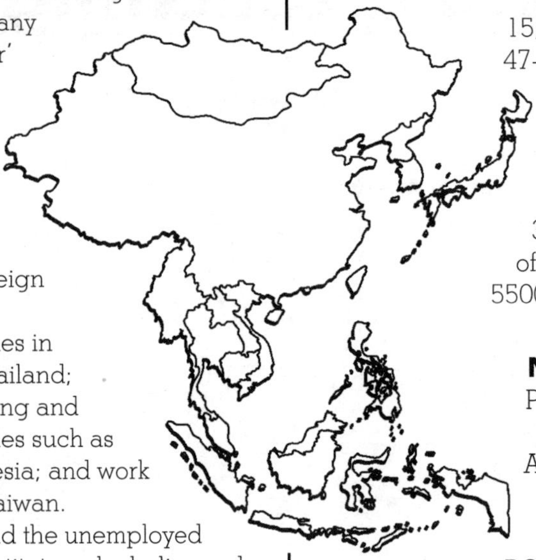

OMF workers plant churches in Japan, the Philippines and Thailand; teach English, music, computing and many other subjects in countries such as Cambodia, China and Indonesia; and work in hospitals in Thailand and Taiwan.

They help the homeless and the unemployed in Hong Kong; minister to prostitutes, alcoholics and drug-addicts in Taiwan; look after orphans in Thailand; work on agricultural projects in Mongolia; work closely with the church in places such as Singapore, Korea and Macau; publish books; and teach theology.

OMFers also translate Scripture into various languages; broadcast the gospel on radio and TV; witness to businessmen, students and factory workers; and care for the poor in cities and in rural areas. They teach missionaries' children; work in mission homes, and serve as dorm-parents, secretaries, administrators and medical advisers.

OMF provides placements and opportunities for Christians with professional skills such as accountants, agriculturalists, architects, businessmen, computer programmers, economists, engineers, lawyers, lecturers, medics, scientists and teachers. All are welcome in Asia. With OMF's help, Christians with these and other qualifications can make valuable contributions to countries such as Cambodia, China, Indonesia, Laos, Mongolia, Myanmar and Vietnam. China alone is looking for 85,000 foreign professionals per year.

Our goal, as in Hudson Taylor's day, is **to glorify God by the urgent evangelisation of East Asia's billions**—telling people about Jesus; teaching, preaching and serving Asians not only throughout Asia but in the UK as well.

For more, see our web site at www.omf.org.uk

English-speaking OMF centres

Australia
PO Box 849
Epping
NSW 1710

Canada
5759 Coopers Avenue
Mississauga
ON L4Z 1R9

Hong Kong
15/F Argyle House
47-49 Argyle Street
Mongkok
Kowloon

Malaysia
3A Jalan Nipah
off Jalan Ampang
55000 Kuala Lumpur

New Zealand
PO Box 10-159
Balmoral
Auckland 1030

Philippines
PO Box 1997-1159
QCCPO
1100 Quezon City

Singapore
2 Cluny Road
Singapore 259570

Southern Africa
P O Box 3080
Pinegowrie 2123
Johannesburg

UK
Station Approach
Borough Green
Sevenoaks
Kent TN15 8BG

USA
10 West Dry Creek Circle
Littleton
CO 80120-4413

OMF International Headquarters
2 Cluny Road
Singapore 259570

Bible

Bible teaching

Contents

Why am I here?

What is this?

A Bible study on Psalm 100, showing that mission is not a goal in itself. The reason God made us, and our purpose in mission, is to worship God.

Why is this question important?

It is essential to have a right emphasis on mission. This means setting our sights right from the start. We want to focus on the greatness of God and see that he alone is worthy of our worship.

Psalm 100 is a call to praise and is intended to be for the whole world. The structure may be broken up into verses 1-3 and then 4-5. Each set of verses parallels the other: a call to praise is followed by a declaration of why the Lord is worthy of praise.

It is only when we have God as the focus of our worship that the rest of our lives fall into place. We mustn't get this the wrong way round. In missions, we mustn't make the *means* (evangelism) more important than the *ends* (God's glory). To lose sight of the goal is to lose our focus and drop our sights.

Psalm 67:4a is a good memory verse. It captures the goal of missions—the gladness of the nations at the greatness of God. One day in heaven, missions and evangelism will no longer be necessary. But worship will last forever.

Worship should be the first step in understanding mission and the fuel and driving force behind it.

Introduction

Imagine meeting the following people:

- An astronaut
- The lead singer of the world's most successful pop group
- The Queen
- The richest person in the world
- Someone who has climbed Mount Everest

Ask the following questions:

- Who would you say is the most famous?
- Who would you most like to meet?
- What do you admire about that person?

We can tell a bit about someone either from what they have made or done. The things which some of these people have done are quite amazing.

The Bible says God made the world and everything in the world—it tells us he spoke the creation into existence. Do you know the most casual verse ever written? It's Genesis 1:16b 'He also made the stars.'

He made you and me too! He made us to have a relationship with him.

Now think about the world around us.

- What does it say about God?
- What do you think we can tell about God from what he has made?
  He is great, powerful, wise, etc
- If God is this great, what should people do?

Bible study

Read Psalm 100 together, or have the children each read a verse. The following questions explore this passage:

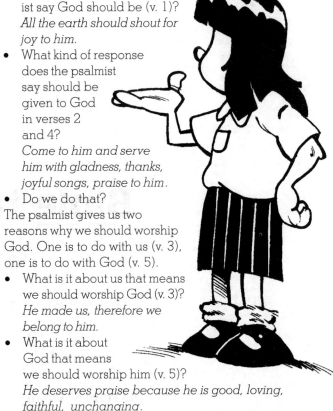

- How famous does the psalmist say God should be (v. 1)?
  All the earth should shout for joy to him.
- What kind of response does the psalmist say should be given to God in verses 2 and 4?
  Come to him and serve him with gladness, thanks, joyful songs, praise to him.
- Do we do that?

The psalmist gives us two reasons why we should worship God. One is to do with us (v. 3), one is to do with God (v. 5).

- What is it about us that means we should worship God (v. 3)?
  He made us, therefore we belong to him.
- What is it about God that means we should worship him (v. 5)?
  He deserves praise because he is good, loving, faithful, unchanging.

I am here so that I can worship God.

Response

People like the Queen are to be respected—if you met her you'd polish up your best manners. The Queen is great, but she didn't make us, and she's not as wonderful as our God. He deserves much more worship than anyone else on earth.

We worship God because he made us and because he deserves it.

- Is this true just on Sundays?

It's true all week long. Worship is not just singing on a Sunday, but is the way we live our lives. So we want to worship God in everything we do all week long. This pleases him.

- Who do you think God wants to worship him?

Everybody that he has made. In response to the good news of all he has done, he wants there to be gladness and songs of joy throughout the whole world. He wants everyone to hear about the new life we can receive through Jesus' death on the cross for us.

Are you ready to pass on the good news? Do you want to see more and more people so glad to know God that they sing for joy?

Memory Verse

Psalm 67:4a 'May the nations be glad and sing for joy.'

Prayer

'Thank you Lord for making me and for looking after me. Thank you that you are a loving and faithful God. Help me give you the thanks that you deserve. Help me tell my friends about you.'

Do my prayers make a difference?

What is this?
A Bible study on the topic of prayer. When we ask in Jesus' name and according to his will, he acts. This is essential to evangelism and mission.

Why is this question important?
Many children are familiar with prayer, in fact they are often very natural pray-ers. Understanding prayer better is vital to learning about our privilege in being involved in God's work in the world.

We want children to understand that Jesus' promises to the disciples apply today, but also that we need to pray into the will of God, not our own selfish desires. We can't manipulate God to our own ends. But he does choose to use us and often waits until we ask before he acts.

This is a good study to put into practice, both in the study-time and privately. See the pages on 'How to pray...' (p 55-58)

Introduction
Do you like to talk with your friends? Wouldn't it be strange if you spent time with them, but never spoke to them?

God wants us to talk with him. That is why we pray. Even though he is God and knows everything, he often waits until we ask before he does something.

Bible Study
Read John 14:13-14.

- What does Jesus tell his friends to do?
  Ask
- Why should we ask if Jesus already knows everything?
  Jesus tells us to

God has given us a very special job of praying, asking him for things. He often waits until we ask before he acts.

- What will Jesus do when they ask?
  Answer; do anything
- Does this mean Jesus will do anything you want him to? Eg burn down your school or make you a millionnaire?

No, Jesus is not a magic genie or a fairy godmother. You cannot make him do anything you want him to. The Bible has many stories of proud people who tried to be the boss instead of obeying God. Can you think of some?

- Finish this sentence from v. 13: Jesus said, 'I will do whatever you ask...' (*in my name*)
- How important are names? Why do we have names?
- If we say, 'Come here [*name of someone in group*]', what part of you do we mean? Just your head, arm, fingernails? (*whole person, not part*)

Do you sometimes finish your prayers, 'in Jesus' name, Amen'? When we think of 'Jesus' name' we are thinking of his whole person. So we need to get to know Jesus and what he is like, so that we can ask for what he would want.

- Jesus gives us a reason why he will answer when we ask. What is the main thing that Jesus wants (v. 13b)?
  Glorify God the Father
- Which of these brings most glory/praise/happiness to God?
  - we obey/disobey him
  - people know him/don't know him
  - people love him/don't love him
  - people trust him/don't trust him

Jesus answers us when we pray for people to know, love, trust and obey God, because this brings glory to God.

Therefore my prayers make a difference because God answers when we ask him for what Jesus wants.

Response
- Do you have friends who don't know and love Jesus? Do you think God would be glorified if they did?
- Does everyone in your street/city/country know and love Jesus? Do you think God would be glorified if they did?
- Does everyone in the world know and love Jesus? Do you think God would be glorified if they did?

Roughly one out of every three people in the world have never heard of Jesus. Many billions of people don't love and trust him.

We must pray for our friends, and for people around the world. We can pray for them 'in Jesus' name' and we know Jesus will answer.

Remember
Although God knows everything, he has told us to ask him for things. He wants to hear us, and he often waits until we ask before he acts.

Sometimes we ask for the wrong things for the wrong reasons. But God always hears and answers. Sometimes he says 'yes', sometimes 'no', and sometimes 'wait.'

We pray in Jesus' name so that his will is done. Then we know it is always for the best.

Memory Verse
John 14:14 'You may ask me for anything in my name, and I will do it.'

Prayer
'Thank you for your gift of prayer. Thank you that you always hear and you always answer. Help us to pray as you want us to. Help us to pray for our friends and people around the world who don't know you yet.'

Do I have to believe in Jesus to go to heaven?

Bible

What is this?

A Bible study focusing on the exclusive claims of Jesus Christ. The context today is of pluralism—the view that all religions are equal and any 'faith' will take you to heaven.

Why is this question important?

People want to have a framework for knowing the truth about life. One of the most comfortable ways of doing this is if everyone finds a truth which is right for them. In today's tolerant world, you can believe what you like, as long as you 'have faith.'

The Bible steers us away from this error. It takes us straight to one fact: Jesus is unique. The Israelites learned early on that God was jealous and would not tolerate other rivals (Exodus 34:14) and he wants whole-hearted devotion from his people (Deut 6.5). The heart of the Christian message is that Jesus—fully God—died for us.

Today's society is similar to that of the early church. In their time, as in ours, there was a spectrum of different religions. The children may have some idea of others in their class at school from various religious backgrounds. We can point to the uniqueness of Jesus among other religious figures:

- He was the only one who claimed to be God
- His death and resurrection verify these claims

Introduction

God made us and wants us to enjoy a relationship with him. He wants us to trust in Jesus and he wants everyone everywhere to know him. Sadly people don't naturally want to follow him. They just want to go their own way. Another sad thing is that one in three people in the world haven't even heard about Jesus.

Bible Study

Read John 14:6. In this verse Jesus tells the disciples how unique he is. He says very clearly that he is the only way back to God the father. Therefore he is the only one who can give people eternal life in heaven.

How would the meaning of this verse be changed if Jesus had said:

- 'I am a way...'
  There are other ways to God than trusting Jesus.
- 'I am a truth...'
  There are other opinions about God that are also true; we don't have to believe Jesus.
- 'I am a life...'
  There are other ways to get new life.

Jesus is the only way, the only truth, the only life and there is no other way to God than through him.

Pic'n'Mix

- Have you ever been to a Pic'n'Mix sweet shop?

Many people today look at life in this way. Just as there are many different kinds of sweets there are many different religions and a lot of people take bits from each. Can you do that?

No, you can't because they believe different things. For example:

- Hindus believe there is a God but we can't know him
- Buddhists believe there is no God
- Muslims believe Allah is God but he is not interested in us
- Some believe God is a force; partly good, partly evil
- Christians believe God is completely good and we can know him

God does not want us to Pic'n'Mix. He wants us to follow him alone and not others.

There is one thing which sets Jesus apart from other religious leaders: he died and then rose again. No one but God has the power over life and death—he is the only true God. That means that the claims that Jesus made about himself being the Son of God are true.

Because he conquered death and rose to life again:

- He can bring us back to God—he is the way
- He is telling the full truth about himself—he is the truth
- He is able to give us life—he is the life

Yes, I do have to believe in Jesus to go to heaven!

Response

The claims Jesus made mean extremely good news! But we don't have all the time in the world. If people throughout the world are to get to heaven they must follow Jesus now. There are so many in the world today who have yet to clearly hear the good news about Jesus in language they can understand.

Christians must get involved in telling others the good news about Jesus, his death on the cross, and God's invitation to heaven.

- How can you be involved in your school, at home or through your church?
- How can you be involved in other countries?

Memory Verse

Acts 4:12 'Salvation is found in no one else, for there is no other name under heaven given to men by which we must be saved.'

Prayer

'Thank you for making yourself known to me. Thank you for dying for me to give me new life. Help me tell others about this new life before it is too late.'

Why should I tell my friends about Jesus?

What is this?

A Bible study looking at the call of Jesus to make disciples, and the part we can play in evangelism.

Why is this question important?

Mission is not just something that somebody else does. It is a universal command from Jesus to all Christians.

Although God's heart for all people is a theme throughout scripture, the 'Great Commission' is a helpful summary. Because the first disciples were faithful in this command, the gospel spread rapidly from Jerusalem. We have the same commission today.

The verses in Matthew 28:18-20 begin with Jesus claiming the total authority of the Godhead. With this in mind, he commands, 'therefore go....' We are ambassadors of Christ. Our mission: to make disciples. We do this by bringing them to saving faith and teaching them to obey.

Some churches may be strong in building up the Christians in the congregation while others place an emphasis on bringing in non-Christians. Both elements need to be strongly present.

Introduction

Trusting Jesus is the only way to please God. We want everyone in the world to know and love Jesus. We're going to think about how we can play our part and tell our friends about him.

Think!

- Have you ever found out some good news and just can't wait to tell others about it?

When we hear good news we can't wait to tell others. Christians want to tell everybody the good news about following Jesus.

- Do you know why people talk about *'famous* last words'?

When you only have one last chance to say someting, you want to say what is most important to you. In the Bible passage, we have the 'famous last words' of Jesus before he went back to heaven. They must be important.

Bible Study

Read Matthew 28:18-20. Here Jesus is talking to his disciples after the resurrection.

- What does v. 18 say about Jesus?
  He is God, he has authority.
- Do you know anyone in authority?
  Teachers, police, parents
- If someone in authority tells you to do something, what do you do?

What Jesus is going to tell us is very important, and we must do what we're told.

- What did Jesus tell his friends to do?
  Go and make disciples
- Where are we told to 'go'? Who should we make into disciples?
  All nations, everyone in the world
- What is a 'disciple'? What two actions are needed? (v. 19b-20a)
  Baptising, teaching them to obey
- What is baptism a sign of?
  Becoming a Christian, that if we decide to follow Jesus, he will wash away our sins and make us clean.
- Why is teaching important?
  Learn how to please and obey God

Making disciples means bringing people to trust Jesus and teaching them to obey him.

- Do you find it easy or hard to tell your friends about Jesus?
- Do you think it is easy for missionaries to go away from home to tell others about Jesus?
- What is Jesus' promise to all of us? (v. 20b)
  He will always be with us

I should tell my friends about Jesus because Jesus told me to. Everyone around the world needs to know Jesus and become his disciple.

Response

We want to tell people the good news about Jesus so that they can love him too. Even if we find this hard, we do it because Jesus commanded us to.

Missionaries are people like you or me who want to obey Jesus' command to make disciples. That's why they go to countries where people need to hear the gospel.

You don't have to go out of your own country to do the same. There are many people where you live who have never heard about Jesus, or who don't love him.

- Think of a friend you know who is not a Christian.
- How can you help him/her to know Jesus?
- Will you pray for him/her this week?

Remember if you find this hard, Jesus promises to be with you and help you.

Memory Verse

Matthew 28:19 'Therefore go and make disciples of all nations, baptising them in the name of the Father and of the Son and of the Holy Spirit.'

Prayer

'Help me to obey your command to make disciples. Thank you that you have given us the privilege of telling other people about you. Thank you that you are always with us.'

Jonah: The Great Escape

Bible

What is this?

A Bible study on Jonah 1. This passage shows God is the maker and ruler of the world, even of people who don't like him!

Why study this passage?

Jonah is an exciting story! Children love both the character Jonah and the experiences he has. This is very useful in helping children to read and enjoy the Bible. But Jonah is much more than just a story. Jesus talks about Jonah twice in the New Testament (see Matthew 12:38 and Luke 11:29-32). He compares his own death 'in the heart of the earth' and Jonah's three days in the fish. But Jesus also refers to him by describing Jonah's ministry as a 'sign.' In Jonah's time, Jesus' time and in our time, God makes truth available to people by sending messengers. Jesus sees Jonah as a preacher. By being a preacher, Jonah points us towards Jesus who showed us God's truth in a complete and unique way.

This book shows God's utter power and control over all things. God chooses to reveal his truth to the people of Nineveh. He must also deal with a reluctant messenger. In this chapter it is God rather than Jonah or the fish who is the important character.

Introduction

We often say people are 'powerful' if they have control over important areas of our lives. Which of the following would you say is the most powerful? What sort of things do they control?

- The head teacher at your school
  How much work you have to do, fun you can/ cannot have
- Different members of your family
  What time you go to bed, what TV you watch
- The boss of McDonald's
  Whether or not you get to eat your favourite food
- The Prime Minister
- What areas are they *not* in control of?
  Eg other countries, the weather, the lottery, nature

This passage shows us all the areas God controls, so we can know he is in charge of everything. As a result we should obey and trust him.

Illustration

Take a normal biro apart and put all the pieces into a small plastic box. Each child is to shake the box as hard as they can until all the pieces have fitted back together. It's almost impossible! Even something as small and simple as a biro needs someone to come along and take time to put it together. Something as large and complex as the world could not have come into being by accident but by God willing it to happen. Jonah is made to understand this, and says that it is God 'who made the land and the sea' (Jonah 1:9).

Bible Study

Read Jonah chapter 1 together or in turns. The children could mime or act out the various parts.

There are many different areas of our lives, and it is sometimes hard to think that God is in charge of them all. In this passage, how does God show he is in control over the following areas?

- Jonah (v. 1-2)?
  Jonah belongs to God, and so can be called or ordered to do whatever God pleases.
- Nineveh (v. 2)?
  All bad acts are known by God as soon as they happen. He knows every detail of how each person behaves. It really matters to him. God wants all people to know about him.
- Nature (v. 4 and 17, also 11-15)?
  Rather than being wild, the sea and weather are governed by God himself. He is able to send a storm and once Jonah is flung out of the boat the storm stops. God also sends the fish to swallow the drowning preacher.
- The sailors who did not know God (v. 10-11, 14, 16)?
  Even though they have never been to Sunday school, the sailors can see from events that God is all-powerful. They are astonished at Jonah's actions and learn to believe and pray themselves.

Response

- Think about the way Jonah behaved on the boat and how that made the sailors feel (v. 10). Is it enough to say you believe in God if you do not act as if you do?
- God chooses us to tell others about him. How do we sometimes try to run away from doing so?
- Are there things we do or think that we try to hide from God?

Memory verse

Jonah 1:9 'I worship the Lord, the God of heaven, who made the sea and the land.'

Prayer

'Thank you Lord that you are in control of everything. Help us to obey you and not run away from what you tell us to do.'

Jonah: The Great Rescue

What is this?

A Bible study on Jonah 2 showing us what we need to be like to please God and for him to be able to use us as his messengers.

Why study this passage?

The first study on Jonah included some remarkable events. For some people, the idea of Jonah ending up inside the stomach of a large fish is hard to swallow—harder perhaps than Jonah was to swallow in the first place! For others, the thought is so vivid it is all they can think about for the rest of the book. We can see why children will want to think about and draw the scene. We must not forget there are three more chapters left. Whether or not we like the idea of spending time inside the whale, we must look at why it was God let this happen to Jonah. This chapter helps us to see that God sent Jonah into the depths to bring him to his knees. Perhaps this was the only way God could make someone as stubborn as Jonah see how dependent he was on God, and finally get around to praying to him.

Jonah had wanted to flee from God (1:3), and now he was face to face with God! By rescuing Jonah from certain death, God shows how loving he is even though people try to ignore or disobey him. God was able to change how Jonah felt about him.

Introduction

What things are you good at? What do you need to be good at to be:

- A member of a famous pop group?
- A rich businessman?
- An astronaut?
- An Olympic gold medal winner?

According to the Bible, the most important thing in life is to be a Christian. What do we need to be good at to be a Christian? God chooses us to tell other people about him. What do we need to be good at for that?

This part of the Bible shows us what God wants us to be like so that we can be most used by him!

Bible Study

Read Jonah 2 together. This chapter is actually a prayer in which Jonah thinks about what has happened to him. He tells God how it has changed him and what he has learnt.

- In verse 3, where does Jonah say he is?
  Drowning in the depths of the sea.
- Jonah understands what this means in verse 4a. Where is he in relation to God?
  He has been sent away from the presence of God.

We can see God is rescuing Jonah from more than the sea—he could have used a lifeboat for that!

- Have you ever wanted something, only to change your mind after finding out what it is really like?

In chapter 1, Jonah disobeyed God by trying to run away. Now he knows how painful it is to be far from God.

- How does he describe what it's like to be away from God (v. 2)?
  Jonah describes it as being in distress, and like being in a grave.
- What does Jonah do now he's in this situation (v. 2)?
  He prays to God.

Jonah has seen how important it is to be close to God. This is a great change in Jonah. During the time trying to run away from God, his boat had been caught in a storm. When the captain asked Jonah to pray, he refused (1:6-7). Now he knows how important God is to life.

- What did God have to do to Jonah to make him want to pray again?
  God had to bring Jonah to the point of death.

In verse 7, even though Jonah was praying from deep in the ocean, his prayer was heard right up in heaven!

- How does God respond to the prayer of Jonah (v. 6b)?
  God rescues Jonah!

'Idols' in verse 8 can be anything which we swap for the importance of God.

- How does verse 8 describe what Jonah had done in the last chapter?
  He thought that his own plans were more important than God's.

Response

God had chosen Jonah to tell the people in Nineveh about him. The one thing we have to be good at to be useful to God is knowing how important he is. God is so important we depend on him for everything, even if we do not know it at the time. The most important lesson for us to learn is that only God can change the way we feel about him. If like Jonah we think we can do what we want all the time, then God may force us to think again.

Memory Verse

Jonah 2:9b 'What I have vowed I will make good. Salvation comes from the Lord.'

Prayer

'Dear Lord, we thank you that you want us to change into people who will follow you.'

Jonah: The Great Turn

What is this?

A Bible study on Jonah 3, showing how God is able to change the way the Ninevites feel about him, and what they do as a result.

Why study this passage?

Having had his relationship with God restored, Jonah is sent to speak to the people of Nineveh for a second time. After all he has been through, there is no question of Jonah saying no as he did in chapter 1. We saw in the last study how God makes Jonah realise his dependence on him. Now understanding more about the power and care of God, he is ready to be a preacher.

Many people are unhappy with many things in the world today and are often not short of suggestions as to what God should be doing! This chapter gives us a clear picture of what God wants to do among the peoples of his world. From the Ninevites' response we see how God wants people to behave. The most important thing is the state of our hearts.

Introduction

- Have you ever wanted to change the world? If you had power to do anything, what sort of things would you change?

The first chapter of Jonah showed us God has all the power there is to have! When he rescued Jonah from death, we saw that he is also caring, and wants people to know him. In this part of Jonah, we see how God has decided to change the world.

Bible Study

God has chosen Jonah to help him change the world! The city God wants Jonah to work in is called Nineveh.

- What sort of place is it (v. 3)?
  It is very important! The Bible tells us it would take you three days to get from one side of the city to the other. Either it is very large, or the traffic is very bad!

At this point, we might expect God to give Jonah special powers or at least a funky costume to do the job of changing such a big place...

- What does Jonah have to do in verse 1?
  He has to give the Ninevites a message.

When was the last time you watched the news? How did it make you feel? Were you happy, sad or just bored? The great surprise for us is that the way God wants to change the world is by *news*. If this news is going to change a whole city, it must be very powerful!

- What is the top story in Jonah's news flash?
  God will punish/overturn Nineveh in 40 days.

Though Jonah is doing the speaking, the Ninevites realise the message has come from God (v. 5a).

Sackcloth was what people in Nineveh used to wear when they were unhappy with themselves. They must have been very sad because they even gave up eating for a while.

- Believing God's news involved more than feeling sad. What else did the Ninevites do (v. 10a)?
  They turned from their evil ways.
- Who acted this way (v. 5b)?
  All of them! From the greatest to the least.

This shows that God's message is for everyone! All sorts of people, rich and poor, realised what they had been doing was wrong. The news worked. It made them change.

- How did this make God feel (v. 10)?
  He had compassion and did not destroy them.

Response

We see God able to be friends with the Ninevites once they had changed. The Bible shows we are all like the Ninevites in not loving God as we should.

- Has the news of God changed your heart?
- Look again at how the Ninevites felt in v. 7-9. How should knowing that we upset God make us feel?

This passage shows that God's news really can change the world!

- How can we be part of God's news team?
- How should we pray for our friends who don't know God, and our church leaders?

Memory Verse

Jonah 3:10 'When God saw what they did and how they turned from their evil ways, he had compassion and did not bring upon them the destruction he had threatened.'

Prayer

'Thank you Lord that you want to change the world. Help us take the good news about becoming your friends to all the different types of people around us.'

Jonah: The Great Sulk

Bible

What is this?
A Bible study on Jonah 4, showing that God's plans are best, even if we do not always understand them.

Why study this passage?
Jonah 4 is not the ending we expect! After the great success at Nineveh we find Jonah so angry with God he wants to die—hardly a normal hero's reaction! We need to understand why Jonah was so upset. He is a constant reminder to us of our human weakness, even with evidence of God's goodness all around him. We mustn't trivialise his complaints. If Jonah can fail at the last hurdle, so can we.

Jonah did not fully understand the message he was preaching. He assumed God would destroy Nineveh whether the people changed their attitudes or not. He did not realise the promised destruction was only the natural consequence of their behaviour at the time. When God showed compassion, Jonah thought he was being inconsistent. Jonah couldn't depend on a God who kept changing his mind. It seemed wrong to spare a people who had been so evil.

The passage shows us God's response. He is not inconsistent, but forgiving. If he can spare a Jonah, he can spare a Ninevite. God owns the whole world (even a vine!), and so he has the final say on who he will forgive.

Introduction
Has anyone ever said, 'you'll catch a cold if you do that!'? Perhaps you were in the rain without a coat, or out in the snow without a scarf, and they wanted to warn you that you might catch a cold.

- What are people wanting you to do when they warn you of something?
  They want you to stop what you are doing so you will be safe.
- If you ignored the person who warned you about catching a cold, what would happen?
  You'd get the sniffles!
- What other things might you warn someone about? What would they need to do about it?

The reason for warning someone about something is so that they avoid the trouble they are heading for. The warning is meant to show them what will happen if they do not stop what they are doing.

In the last study, God warned the people of Nineveh through Jonah. If they carried on displeasing God then in 40 days they would be punished. We saw how the Ninevites listened carefully and changed what they were doing.

This is the last part of the story, and we will see from Jonah how easy it is to think that we know better than God, even when we are friends with him!

Bible Study
Read Jonah 4 together. The children could mime or act out the various parts.

Jonah does not like the Ninevites.

- Why is he so angry with God (v. 1-2)?
  God has not destroyed the Ninevites.

Jonah has not seen what the warning had been meant to do. He hoped God would destroy the city in 40 days whatever happened. God's plan was different. He wanted the Ninevites to be careful and so he warned them.

- Are there people we would not want God to be friends with?

Look again at the story about the vine (v. 5-9)

- Why was Jonah wrong to be angry (v. 10-11)?
  God owns both the vine and the city, and so can do what he thinks is best with them.

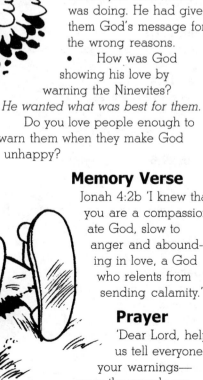

Think again of someone warning you about catching a cold. Imagine you wrapped up warmly because of the warning and didn't catch a cold. It would be strange if this made the person who had warned you angry! That is just what Jonah was doing. He had given them God's message for the wrong reasons.

- How was God showing his love by warning the Ninevites?
  He wanted what was best for them.
- Do you love people enough to warn them when they make God unhappy?

Memory Verse
Jonah 4:2b 'I knew that you are a compassionate God, slow to anger and abounding in love, a God who relents from sending calamity.'

Prayer
'Dear Lord, help us tell everyone your warnings—even the people we don't like. We thank you that you love all people.'

More memory verses

Bible

Old Testament

Psalm 22:27
All the ends of the earth will remember and turn to the Lord, and all the families of the nations will bow down before him.

Psalm 57:9-11
I will praise you, O Lord, among the nations; I will sing of you among the peoples. For great is your love, reaching to the heavens; your faithfulness reaches to the skies. Be exalted, O God, above the heavens; let your glory be over all the earth.

Psalm 67:1-2
May God be gracious to us and bless us and make his face shine upon us, that your ways may be known on earth, your salvation among all nations.

Psalm 96:3
Declare his glory among the nations, his marvelous deeds among all peoples.

Psalm 96:5
For all the gods of the nations are idols, but the Lord made the heavens.

Psalm 102:15
The nations will fear the name of the Lord, all the kings of the earth will revere your glory.

Psalm 105:1
Give thanks to the Lord, call on his name; make known among the nations what he has done.

Psalm 117:1
Praise the Lord, all you nations; extol him, all you peoples.

Isaiah 12:4
In that day you will say: 'Give thanks to the Lord, call on his name; make known among the nations what he has done, and proclaim that his name is exalted.'

Isaiah 49:6
It is too small a thing for you to be my servant to restore the tribes of Jacob and bring back those of Israel I have kept. I will also make you a light for the Gentiles, that you may bring my salvation to the ends of the earth.

Isaiah 66:19
I will set a sign among them, and I will send some of those who survive to the nations... and to the distant islands that have not heard of my fame or seen my glory. They will proclaim my glory among the nations.

Jonah 2:8
Those who cling to worthless idols forfeit the grace that could be theirs.

New Testament

Matthew 9:37-38
Then he said to his disciples, 'The harvest is plentiful but the workers are few. Ask the Lord of the harvest, therefore, to send out workers into his harvest field."

Matthew 28:19a
Go and make disciples of all nations.

Luke 24:46-47
He told them, 'This is what is written: The Christ will suffer and rise from the dead on the third day, and repentance and forgiveness of sins will be preached in his name to all nations, beginning at Jerusalem.'

Acts 1:8
But you will receive power when the Holy Spirit comes on you; and you will be my witnesses in Jerusalem, and in all Judea and Samaria, and to the ends of the earth.

Acts 13:47
For this is what the Lord has commanded us: 'I have made you a light for the Gentiles, that you may bring salvation to the ends of the earth.'

Romans 10:13-15
'Everyone who calls on the name of the Lord will be saved.' How, then, can they call on the one they have not believed in? And how can they believe in the one of whom they have not heard? And how can they hear without someone preaching to them? And how can they preach unless they are sent? As it is written, 'How beautiful are the feet of those who bring good news!'

Galatians 3:8
The Scripture foresaw that God would justify the Gentiles by faith, and announced the gospel in advance to Abraham: 'All nations will be blessed through you.'

Revelation 5:9
And they sang a new song: 'You are worthy to take the scroll and to open its seals, because you were slain, and with your blood you purchased men for God from every tribe and language and people and nation.'

Revelation 7:9-10
After this I looked and there before me was a great multitude that no one could count, from every nation, tribe, people and language, standing before the throne and in front of the Lamb. They were wearing white robes and were holding palm branches in their hands. And they cried out in a loud voice: 'Salvation belongs to our God, who sits on the throne, and to the Lamb.'

What's it like?

Contents

What's it like? My first week in Asia – 1

What is it?

Discussion questions to go with postcards giving children an idea of what it's like going to a new country, learning a new language and facing culture shock.

What will they learn?

The problems new workers face:

- Learning to speak a different language (greetings, sentences, conversations)
- Learning new customs (showing respect, getting up times, social visits)
- Learning how to do practical things (count money, buy things)
- Coping without family, friends, favourite foods, fellowship

What do you do?

Photocopy and hand out the diary (p 19). Ask for volunteers to read out loud the story for each day.

Use the questions below to involve the children and make them think about what's going on.

Questions to ask

Day 1

- Have you ever been the new person (eg in school) having to learn who everyone is?
- What feelings did you have at first?
  Lonely, embarrassed, confused
- What did people do that helped/didn't help?
- How long was it before you felt you belonged?
- What would it be like if you couldn't speak their language?
- What greetings do you know in other languages?

Day 2

Every country has rules/customs for how people should behave.

- What are the polite things we are taught to do?
  Say 'please' and 'thank you', put up your hand if you want to speak in class, open doors for others...
- How do you learn these things?
  From family, teachers, by copying others, being praised when you do them and punished when you don't!

Day 3

- What are your favourite foods?
- What food do you think you would miss if you lived overseas?

There are often lots of new and interesting things to eat in other countries (see Snacks section for further ideas, p 87)

Day 4

Show children British coins and notes and do some counting.

Show any holiday money (foreign currency) you have. Let children handle it and ask questions. Notice the different colours, sizes and shapes of coins and notes.

Other ideas

- 'A care package' (p 54) — sending a parcel to your missionary
- 'At the market stall' (p 81) — trying to haggle/bargain with play money
- 'I packed my bag...' (p 78) — a memory game that doesn't need any preparation.
- 'Toilet game' (p 79) — illustrates the perils of not knowing the language!
- Snacks (p 87) — give the children a taste of something completely different

How can we pray for new missionaries?

- See 'How to pray for new missionaries' (p 55)
- Pray with the children for missionaries they know

My first week in Asia – 1

Day 1 Monday

It's been an exciting day starting work, but boy is my arm sore—shaking so many hands! The people are very friendly and always stop to say 'how are you?' in their language. I can now reply quite quickly and with another 200 practices tomorrow, I should get even faster! There are so many new names and faces to remember—how will I do it?

Day 2 Tuesday

Its been really hot today and everyone is munching on icepops—even the grownups!! I'm trying to get a suntan so I won't stick out in the crowd so much. (Getting stared at a lot makes you feel like a weirdo.) I was really insulted when my neighbour greeted me saying 'you are looking very fat today!' Because I was still cross thinking about this, I accidentally did a terrible thing on my way to work—I didn't stand up to let an older person take my seat in the crowded bus. There are so many things to remember to do, that I forgot this rule for showing respect to your elders.

Day 3 Wednesday

Last night I dreamt about eating a box of Maltesers and prayed for a parcel of goodies to come from home. I've also been dreaming about cornflakes. Black rice porridge is not my favourite dish for breakfast. As well as food, I'm beginning to miss my friends and family. Everyone here seems to belong to a big family with lots of uncles, cousins, grandparents etc. They all live together. I feel a bit lonely now, but my new friend at work is taking me to church this Sunday. Oh—she explained that to call someone 'fat' is really a compliment and means you are looking healthy and properly fed!

Day 4 Thursday

I saw some children playing football in their flipflops—hope they don't break a toe. The nearest hospital is miles away! Today I spotted another curious thing. A woman took off her shoe in a shop, bent down and picked out some coins—that's handier than carrying a purse isn't it? I'm finding sorting out the money a real pain! I can't read what is written on the paper notes. Guessing the value by their colour doesn't always work when they are really dirty.

What's it like? My first week in Asia – 2

What is it?

More discussion questions to go with postcards giving children an idea of what it's like going to a new country, learning a new language and facing culture shock.

What will they learn?

The problems new workers face:

- Learning to speak a different language (greetings, sentences, conversations)
- Learning new customs (showing respect, getting up times, social visits)
- Learning how to do practical things (count money, buy things)
- Coping without family, friends, favourite foods, fellowship

What do you do?

Photocopy and hand out the diary (p 21). Ask for volunteers to read the story from each day out loud.

Use the questions below to involve the children and make them think about what's going on.

Questions to ask

Day 5

- What are your favourite TV programmes?
- Which would you miss most if you lived overseas?
- Did you know...? In Indonesia you can watch Premier League football live at 9.00pm?

Day 6

- How do you know how much to pay for something? *See the price tag.*

In many countries, there are no price tags. You and the shopkeeper have to agree to a price. You want to get it cheap. The shopkeeper wants to make it expensive.

For example: The seller names the starting price of 20p for a chocolate bar. You offer 10p (which is about half the asking price). The seller will say this is the best chocolate he has ever seen. The buyer will say it tastes rotten. Eventually they will reach an agreed price about half way between the two figures. The buyer hopes it'll be 14p, the seller hopes for 16p!

To play at shops see 'At the market stall' (p 81)

Day 7

Talk about God as our heavenly Father—which means we are his children. We have relatives—brothers and sisters in Christ who live all over the world. We belong to the universal church.

Other ideas

- 'A care package' (p 54) — sending a parcel to your missionary
- 'At the market stall' (p 81) — trying to haggle/bargain with play money
- 'I packed my bag...' (p 78) — a memory game that doesn't need any preparation.
- 'Toilet game' (p 79) — illustrates the perils of not knowing the language!
- Snacks (p 87) — give the children a taste of something completely different

How can we pray for new missionaries?

- See 'How to pray for new missionaries' (p 55)
- Pray with the children for missionaries they know

My first week in Asia – 2

Day 5 Friday

What do you think arrived today? A parcel! I could hardly wait to rip it open—inside there was a box of Crunchy Nut Cornflakes and I hugged it! But would you believe, when I tore open the lid I found not cornflakes but a woolly hat, scarf and glove set (which isn't very practical in this heat!) There was a letter and that cheered me up reading all the news from home and finding out who'd won Wimbledon. It seems strange having no TV here, but I'm so busy I don't really miss it. Yet!

Day 6 Saturday

I'd planned to have a long lie-in this morning, but my neighbour (who said that nice thing about me being fat) woke me up at 5.30am to come in for a chat. She must think I'm really lazy staying in bed after sunrise. I enjoyed her visit but will I ever get used to these early starts? Good job I have a loud alarm clock!

Later on, I went to buy bananas in the market. This was my first attempt at bargaining with a seller. I felt a bit embarrassed and scared, but I remembered how to say the phrase 'its too expensive' and kept repeating this. The seller laughed a lot (maybe I said it wrong?). Anyway, it was a friendly fight and we were both happy when the sale was successful.

Day 7 Sunday

My friend took me to church early this morning. I found it hard to sit still for the whole service as I didn't understand what was being said. I missed singing choruses, but the new songs I heard were nice too. Suddenly I realised here is the big family I'd been wanting. Here we were worshipping God together as his children.

What's it like? A missionary kid – 1

What is it?

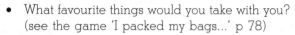

Discussion questions to use with letters from a missionary kid in boarding school.

What will they learn?

The problems missionary kids face:

- Separation from parents—loneliness, missing mum when sick, responsibilities

The benefits missionary kids have:

- Fun and friendships, adults who make them feel special

What do you do?

Preparation

- Photocopy and hand out the letters (p 23) to each child

OR

- Cut out the individual letters. Put in separate envelopes, seal and hand out to three children (mark the number clearly on the front of each one).

On the day

- Have the letters read out in order
- Use the questions below to involve the children in the missionary kids' situation.
- The questions could be used before or after reading the letters.

Letter 1

The journey to boarding school can take a whole day or overnight.

- Tell me about a long journey you've been on. Imagine if you had to leave your family for four months to go to school. How would you feel?

- What favourite things would you take with you? (see the game 'I packed my bags...' p 78)

Letter 2

Highlight the similarities between the children and missionary kids:

- What do you like to do after school? What pets do you have?
- What instrument are you learning to play?
- Do you say prayers at night time? (see 'How to pray for missionary kids' p 56)

Letter 3

The problem of coping with a missing pet is made more difficult being away from home.

- Who has a bedroom on their own? Who shares? Which is best?
- What would sharing it with 11 other people be like?
- What would be the advantages/disadvantages? *Never alone in the dark/time for lights out/no privacy*

Making their beds quickly is just one thing missionaries' children have to do at school. They have other jobs too like looking after younger brothers and sisters. They don't get as much individual attention as in a family situation.

- What jobs do you do to help your parents?

Other ideas

- 'I packed my bag...' (p 78) — a memory game that doesn't need any preparation
- A pop-up card (p 67) — make a snake card
- Origami craft (p 70-72) — make a plane or a frog using this Japanese paper craft
- 'How to pray for missionary kids' (p 56)
- Kids like me — Onka Shooey (p 50)

Dear mum & dad – 1

Letter 1

Dear mum & dad,

my ears hurt in the plane, but they popped later and then I was OK. We met up with some of our friends in Kuala Lumpur, I was really excited! We'd two months news to tell each other. Tim got car sick and we had to stop the taxi on the windy road. Little brothers can be embarrassing. It took us five hours to get up the hill and then we arrived back at our school in the jungle! Some of us felt a bit homesick for a couple of nights, but we feel better now. I miss you both,

love Jo xx

Letter 2

Dear mum & dad,

the pony, goats, cats and the naughty dog—Sandy, are still here. We've also got another dog called Pooch to keep her company. Pooch is very friendly. He wags his tail a lot! Sandy has had obedience lessons and can shake hands (with her paw) and sit when you tell her to. I love riding my bike during playtime. Miss Gordon is a new teacher here—she's staying for one year. She's teaching some of us to play the guitar. Tim fell and cut his knee yesterday. His Dorm Auntie put a plaster on it. When he was tucked up in bed with teddy, I told him how much God loves and cares for him. Then we said our prayers together.

lots of lurve Jo xo

Letter 3

Dear dad & mum

when my Dorm Auntie (Diane) read your letter to me, I wanted to fly home and help look for my missing rabbits. Did George and Pistol escape through the hole in the fence? I hope you find them! Twelve of us sleep in Auntie Diane's dorm. It was my turn to sit on her knee during the Sunday Special meeting. She's my special person and gives our whole dorm treats on Sunday afternoons. We had marshmallows and popcorn yesterday—delicious!!! Tim can now tie his own shoelaces (but I usually help him if they come loose while he's playing). He hates making his bed and is always grumpy when he wakes up.

love Jo xox

What's it like? A missionary kid – 2

What is it?
More discussion questions to use with letters home from a missionary kid in boarding school.

What will they learn?
The problems missionary kids face:
- Separation from parents—loneliness, coping with a bully, having pets die

The benefits missionary kids have:
- Big and small group fun activities, outdoor adventure, anticipation of family reunions

What do you do?
Preparation
- Photocopy and hand out the letters (p 25) to each child

OR
- Cut out the individual letters. Put in separate envelopes, seal and hand out to three children (mark the number clearly on the front of each one).

On the day
- Have the letters read out in order
- Use the questions below to involve the children in the missionary kids' situation.
- The questions could be used before or after reading the letters.

Letter 4
You get bullies in most schools.
- What kind of things do bullies do at your school?
- When bullying happens who can you tell?
  Teachers, parents, friends, church leaders
- Who could Jo talk to?
  Could also write/e-mail home

Note: Bullying can be a sensitive issue for some who may be experiencing similar problems at school. Please give advice carefully and sensitively.

Letter 5
- What might you find in a jungle?
  Plants, animals, insects

Have some library books on hand to discover which wild animals live in different parts of East Asia or make a pop-up snake card (see p 67)

Letter 6
Explain that all missionary kids go home to their parents for Christmas.
- What do you think Christmas is like for missionary kids in Asia?
- How does your family celebrate Christmas? Make a list.
- What things on that list could/couldn't a missionary family do?
- What might they eat on Christmas day?
  Not usually turkey! Sometimes families have special treats like sausages and baked beans that they couldn't normally buy!
- Why don't you try doing some origami too?

Other ideas
- 'I packed my bag...' (p 78) — a memory game that doesn't need any preparation
- A pop-up card (p 67) — make a snake card
- Origami craft (pp 70-72) — make a plane or a frog using this Japanese paper craft
- 'How to pray for missionary kids' (p 56)
- Kids like me — Onka-Shooey (p 50)

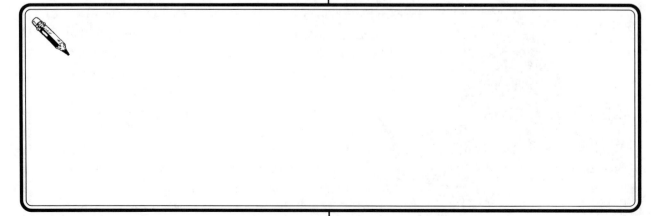

Dear mum & dad – 2

Letter 4

Dear mumzo & dadzo,

half-term was fantastic fun! We watched 'Charlie and the Chocolate Factory' on video. We were all given some bars of chocolate. There were two golden tickets hidden inside the wrappers. I was one of the lucky ones to get a ticket!!! My prize was brill—I got a little truck full of miniature chocolate bars and shared some with my friends and with Tim. One naughty girl tried to take some of my bars. She is a bully and annoys most of the smaller kids. It's hard trying to avoid her as we are always here together. Our teachers spend time with us even when we aren't in class. They are more like friends or parents to us (of course I'd rather have you).

love Jo ox

Letter 5

Dear mum & dad,

Pooch has gone missing—we went into the jungle to look for him, but he's disappeared. My friend Ali says he's been gobbled up by a tiger! We saw some yellow bellies (harmless snakes) and monkeys, but didn't meet any tigers—I had my penknife ready anyway. I love going on hikes in the jungle. We usually take a picnic. Auntie Diane told us a creepy story about goblins drinking out of the monkey cups that grow on trees—we enjoyed the scary bits.

luv Jo x

Letter 6

Dear mum & dad,

Ali and I have joined the origami club this term, we are making—sorry, I can't tell you, it would spoil the surprise as it's your Christmas present! The model town has been set up in the hall. We can look at it every day. There's a train track, lights and little people—I like them the best.

Have any Christmas parcels arrived from granny and grandpa? Only four more days to go to the end of term—I can't wait to be with you again

trillions of tons of love Jo xxx

What's it like?
An English teacher in China

What is it?

A day in the life of an English teacher in China, giving children an idea of what it's like to work there as a Christian.

What will they learn?

The challenges and joys of helping Chinese students find out more about Jesus.

What do you do?

- Photocopy the story (p 27)
- Give each child a copy and you read the light type
- Invite all the children to join in with the exclamations in bold type

OR

- Use helpers to act out the story as you read

Introduction

The Chinese government bans missionaries but they allow Christians from overseas to come and do jobs to help China develop. There are openings in all sorts of jobs from pastry making to expert farming. By far the biggest demand is for English teachers. Here is a little peep into a day in the life of one of them.

Scene 1

- Why do you think the teacher makes a joke about the rats?
  He probably hates them coming into his flat but joking about it helps him cope. A sense of humour is very important for people living overseas.

Scene 2

- Why does the teacher let Li Hua help him?
  He doesn't want to be a big head. He wants to be good at making friends.

Scene 3

- Will the prayers of the old lady ever work from so far away?
  Just wait and see!

Scene 4

- Why do the students like the teacher eating the Chinese sweeties?
  It shows he loves China and feels at home there. He is growing closer to the Chinese people.

Scene 5

- Why is Wang Dong's supper the last thing on his mind tonight?
  He realises only Jesus can save him from his sins and he doesn't want to put it off any longer.

Scene 6

- Why does the teacher not send his visitors away so he can have his supper in peace.
  He wants to be kind to his students. The way he behaves shows them what Jesus is like. After what happened to Wang Dong, a rumbly tummy and a mess on the carpet don't seem to matter!

Bible reference

1 Timothy 1:15 'Here is a trustworthy saying that deserves full acceptance: Christ Jesus came into the world to save sinners—of whom I am the worst.'

What else to say

If we were in China today we'd be breaking the law by meeting together like this. No-one under 18 is allowed to learn about God. That means 500 million boys and girls like Wang Li Bing (p 46). There are no Sunday schools, no Scripture Unions, no holiday Bible clubs, no prayers or Bible readings at school assembly. In school children are taught there is no God who is great, only the Chinese people are great.

- Ask the children to pray for more Christian teachers from the UK to go and work in China.
  The children may be overjoyed at the thought of their own teacher going to China!
- How might they decide what they want to do when they grow up?
  Something they enjoy/are good at, a job that pays a lot of money
- Challenge them to think about what God wants them to do—maybe even go to China!

Other ideas

You could also include:

- Kids like me — Wang Li Bing (p 46)
- Game — 'Wakey, wakey' (p 78)
- Game — Shoe scramble (p 79)
- Make 'Chinese streamers' (p 66)
- Cook a Chinese recipe (p 88)
- Use 'How to pray for Asian non-Christians' (p 58)

What's it like? An English teacher in China

Scene 1 — Early one winter morning...

Very early, in fact! (**yawn, yawn**) 6 o'clock and the college loud speakers have just gone off. It's the wakey, wakey call. Time for my Chinese students to drag themselves out of bed and hurry to the playground for their morning exercises. No-one can be late. Thankfully the teachers don't have to join in (**that's me!**). I can huddle under my big duvet for a few more blissful minutes (**ahhh!**). It's freezing outside (**brrr!**)

Oh no! As I gobble down my rice porridge I notice the holes in my carpet. They're definitely getting bigger. Mr Rat must have been hungry last night. I thought I heard him scratching on the door. But why is it always my flat he wants to nosey around in? (**boo hoo!**) Ling Yen says when the rats see all the chocolate bar wrappers stuck up on my door they think it's a foreign sweetie shop (**yummie!**) and just want to try some new flavours! I wonder what they think of the carpet?!

Scene 2 — Later that morning...

Li Hua spots me at the market and insists on helping (**boo hoo!**).

My Chinese is good enough now to shop on my own and Li Hua is a bit of a bossy boots. I'd rather she left me alone but allowing people to help me is a good way to make friends and besides, God isn't pleased when I get a big head and think I can do things all by myself. Off we go!

At the market Li Hua asks what kind of food I like.

'Oh, everything!' I reply enthusiastically (**aargh!**)

'Pigs ear?' she wonders. These are her favourite.

'A little...' I mutter, not wanting to offend her.

Fortunately the market are out of fresh ones. (**Phew!**) What a relief.

Scene 3 — After lunch...

Ah great! Two whole hours to read my Bible and pray before my next class (**yippee!**). I won't have any interruptions because all the students are in bed taking a nap and trying to keep warm!

Every week I teach about 200 students in English classes. That's a lot of names to learn and an awful lot to pray for. It takes me ages.

Yesterday I got a letter from an old lady who lives a long way away in Tipperary. I think she's nearly 90. Guess what. She prays for my students too, that they'd come to know Jesus. She's expecting to see them all in heaven eventually (**wow!**). She gets quite excited about it all even though she's nearly 90. With ladies like that around you just never know what will happen next.

Scene 4 — That same afternoon...

On the way home from class I go into the corner shop for some sweets. A few of the students follow me. They think I'll buy the foreign bubble-gum but instead I go for the Chinese preserved plums (**ha, ha!**). They're my favourite! The students have a great laugh and say I'm just like a Chinese person now (**cool!**).

Scene 5 — Just before supper...

Back in my flat I'm still sucking the life out of my last preserved plum when there's a quiet tap at the door. (**Who can this be?**) The tin rice bowls are clattering outside. Most students are rushing to the canteen to be first in the queue for supper. I open the door and there is Wang Dong, looking nervous and shy and not very hungry at all. He comes straight in, refuses a cup of tea (**shock horror!**), and tells me something is seriously wrong. The words blurt out,

'All term I've felt like the worst man in the world. Only Jesus can help me now.'

Talk about a surprise (**wow!**). I could have swallowed my chopsticks! Wang Dong has been secretly tuning into a radio programme about the Bible. Now he wants to become a Christian! (**Yippee!**)

'In the Bible Mr Paul says Christ Jesus came into the world to save sinners. Is that true?' asks Wang Dong.

'Yes, yes!' I say and his worried face breaks into a big smile. Makes you think he's hearing the best news of his life (**and he is!**). Just wait until Tipperary hears about this! God did hear those prayers!

Scene 6 — Later that night...

There's a loud knock at the door. Fan Ping and her friend come in to borrow my Bash Street Kids annual.

Two minutes later there's another knock at the door and five more students come in to show me their prize stamp collections. We drool over them together.

Liu Dong Ping arrives next wearing a black armband and tells me his goldfish has died (**boo, hoo!**). A few minutes later, another knock on the door and eight first year girls come tumbling in to show me the new high-heeled wellington boots they've bought for the rainy season. By the time everyone has gone I've made Chinese tea for 16 people, there is orange peel all over the carpet and I still haven't had my supper (**rumble, rumble**).

So what. Today in China something happened. Something mega. God made it happen and I was there.

Goodnight. (**Snore... snore...**)

Bobby gets ready for a special job in Japan

What is it?

A testimony linked to birthdays showing how God got a boy from Liverpool ready for a job in Japan.

What will they learn?

- How Bobby became a Christian and started to serve God in his local church
- Why he gave up his dreams with Liverpool Football Club to become a missionary in Japan

What do you need?

- Birthday cake(s). Make sure you have enough to give everyone a slice
- 18 candles
- Box of matches
- Knife
- Plates or serviettes

What do you do?

- Read the story to the children. The narrator dresses up in a football strip and pretends to be Bobby
- As each part is finished light the appropriate number of candles. Choose a child to blow them out, then go on to the next part
- When the story is over cut the cake and share it out!

Bible references

- **1 Samuel 16:7** 'Man looks at the outward appearance, but the Lord looks at the heart.'
- **Isaiah 53:5** 'But he was pierced for our transgressions, he was crushed for our iniquities; the punishment that brought us peace was upon him, and by his wounds we are healed.'
- **Revelation 7:9-10** 'After this I looked and there before me was a great multitude that no-one could count, from every nation, tribe, people and language, standing before the throne and in front of the Lamb. They were wearing white robes and were holding palm branches in their hands. And they cried out in a loud voice:

  "Salvation belongs to our God,
  who sits on the throne,
  and to the Lamb."'

Other ideas

- Find out if there are overseas students or workers living near you. Do they have any children? Discuss ways of making friends with them and telling them about Jesus
- Find out what it's like to be a young person in Japan. See Hashimoto (p 44)
- Ask what they want to be when they grow up. Show that following God's plan for your life is the most exciting of all

Bobby gets ready for a special job in Japan

8th birthday

Had my eighth birthday party today. All my friends came. We stuffed ourselves on chocolate cake (mum decorated it in Liverpool colours). We all went out the back and played football. It's late now and everyone's gone home. I should be asleep but I've been tossing and turning all night and thinking lots about God and about church and about our minister's wife. You see, I think she's got it wrong. Every Sunday she says something to mum and dad about what good boys they've got (that's me and Jimmy, my little brother) or about what little angels we are (or something equally soppy!). I just think she's got it totally wrong. I mean, I don't think God would agree with her. If he knows all about me like he says he does then he sees all that selfishness and meanness in me. He knows what I'm really like even better than Jimmy does! Lying in bed now God's watching me and there's no hiding. I can't get these words from the Bible out of my head,

'Man looks on the outside but God looks on the heart.' What am I going to do?

9th birthday

A few months ago everything just seemed to fit together. I was reading in Isaiah 53. It says that on the cross God put the punishment for my sin on Jesus instead of me and I can be safe. Wow! What a rescue plan. I really needed to hear that and then I needed to ask God to rescue ME and he has! I blew out the candles on my cake today and made a wish that some day I'd do something great for God with my life. I'm so excited I can't get to sleep!

16th birthday

I'm old enough now to apply for a summer outreach team. Great, or so I thought. I put down Belfast as my first choice. It sounded quite dangerous and I fancy myself as a bit of an action hero. But guess what. They're sending me on a beach mission to Blackpool instead. A beach doesn't sound very adventurous at all! I'm so disappointed. I had a good talk with my dad and he says God won't ask us to do big jobs for him if we can't do the small ones well first. I've offered to sweep the floor after the church youth club on Saturday nights. That means every Saturday night right through the winter even when I've had a really hard football match that afternoon. I know it's going to be tough but I want to stick at it.

17th birthday

Last week an important man from Liverpool Football Club came round to our house. He talked to mum and dad about me joining them for two years. Everybody up our street is excited. They think I'm going to be the next Michael Owen! Ha, ha. This year, as well as everything else that's been happening, I've read right through to the end of my Bible. Today the stuff I read blew my mind. It was all about Jesus, not on a cross but on a throne (a very big one, I think). A lot of people from all over the world were standing there in front of the throne, almost rooted to the spot. They couldn't take their eyes off Jesus and were singing about how amazing and great he is. Just thinking about it made the hair on the back of my neck stand up. Then I realised this is actually going to happen when the end of the world comes. People from every nation and language in the world will be there and I'll be there too. Wow!

18th birthday

A Japanese youth team are at Anfield on a summer soccer camp. My coach asked me to help out at some of the training sessions. I'm getting to know them really well. Over the weekend they've been staying with families from our church. Tonight we had a barbeque and they all made origami water bombs and soaked me because it was my 18th birthday. It was a brilliant laugh. We couldn't believe they hadn't heard of Jesus before now. There can't be many Christians in Japan! Jimmy has the youth fellowship praying like mad. We gave them Japanese Bibles and they've started reading them from cover to cover (they don't like skipping over the hard bits). Now I think I know what I want to do with the rest of my life! I have one more year of my contract to do at Liverpool. Then I'm going to Bible college (I sent my application off today) and then Japan!! It'll be three years before I finish Bible college. Then I'll have to learn Japanese. This is the scariest thing I've ever done because I'm not very good at exams. But I just keep thinking of heaven and Jesus on the cross and that big throne and all those people who love him singing their guts out and the Japanese singing being the loudest of all! I never want to go back to normal life after this!

What's it like? A Bible translator in the Philippines – 1

What is it?

Discussion questions to use with postcards from a Bible translator in the Philippines (Roo-Barb) to his home church (St Custards).

What will they learn?

- Bible translators work in remote areas
- How the Christian message is first introduced to people

What do you do?

Preparation

- Make photocopies of the postcards for the children to colour in

OR

- Enlarge the postcards and then photocopy and colour them in
- Glue on to cardboard (cereal boxes)

On the day

- Let different children read the postcards out loud
- Lead discussion based on the following ideas:

Postcard 1

Discuss fitness and learning new skills. *(eg how to swim, ride a motorbike...)*

Draw up a list of useful things for a missionary to know how to do. *(eg repair a puncture, cook...)*

- How does Roo-barb feel when he gets to the village?
  Exhausted, lonely, missing his TV, or happy, excited, eager to meet and chat with his friends again...
- Play the game 'Munch, munch, you're lunch!' (see p 86)

Postcard 2

- Who were these visitors or strangers that came to the village?
  Missionaries.
- Why did they talk about the villager's 'ancient grandpa' idea of God?
  They were starting with what the villagers knew and understood, and building on that.

Read Acts 17:22-31. Paul speaks to the religious men of Athens and tells them the true identity of 'The Unknown God' they had built an idol to. He uses what they are familiar with as a starting point and then tells them about Jesus. Compare the Manobo missionaries' actions to this—how they built on the villagers' belief in a creator god.

- How can we do the same thing in our country?

For your info...

- The Manobo language has three completely separate dialects. 20,000 people speak each dialect
- There are over 150 languages spoken in the Philippines
- The village has approximately 150 people living in it. They are all related to each other going back two generations

Other ideas

- 'Munch, munch, you're lunch!' game (p 86) — to let the children imagine trying to get across the river to the village
- 'How to pray for Asian Christians' and 'How to pray for Asian non-Christians' (pp 57-58)

Teacher's notes

What's it like?

Postcards from the Philippines–1

Postcard 1

Dear St. Custards,

Getting to my village from the city is an adventure! There are no buses going near it, so I ride a motorbike and take a bag on my back. Two and a half hours up the road I have to stop because that's where the road runs out! The next part of the journey is an uphill hike. Two hours of walking is a very sticky business when it's the hottest time of the day. Phew! I'm exhausted when I see my village—only 100 metres away, but I still have the river to cross before I get there! Sometimes the water is only up to my knees and I can easily wade across, but it's usually deeper and sometimes over my head! Then I have to leave my bag on the river bank and swim across (I'm really glad I had those swimming lessons just before I left home!).

From, Roo-Barb

Postcard 2

Dear St Custards,

As you know my village is in a wild part of the countryside, far away from the city. The headman in the village (the BIG BOSS), told me the story of the first visitors. The villagers were pleased to meet these strangers and they all sat down to chat. The strangers asked lots of questions like: who made the world? And who controls everything that happens in it? The headman explained the people in his village believe, 'there is a god who made the world but we don't know him because he doesn't do anything now.' (Just like a very ancient grandpa!) 'There are evil spirits who are really the ones in charge of things. The spirits want to eat human blood, so when someone is sick we kill a chicken and hope that the spirit will be happy with its blood instead of the sick persons. If the spirit accepts the chicken's blood, the sick person gets well again.' He said the strangers left but often came back to visit the village.

The headman began asking what they thought about these things. The visitors told him that they worshipped the God who created the world and that he is still in charge of it. They told him all about God's son called Jesus. Some of the villagers believed and became Christians. Since then the visitors have been busy writing down the villagers' language (it's called Manobo). They have been writing out the words of Jesus for them to read.

From, Roo-Barb

What's it like? A Bible translator in the Philippines – 2

What is it?

More discussion questions to use with postcards from a Bible translator in the Philippines (Roo-Barb) to his home church (St Custards).

What will they learn?

- The lifestyle of village people
- The reason for doing translation work

What do you do?

Preparation

- Make photocopies of the postcards for the children to colour in

OR

- Enlarge the postcards and then photocopy and colour them in
- Glue on to cardboard (cereal boxes)

On the day

- Let different children read the postcards out loud
- Lead discussion based on the following ideas:

Postcard 3

- Can you imagine having no books to read? *Discuss the difficulties for the children going to nursery, then primary and secondary school.*
- Does anyone know how to count to 10 in another language... in five languages!?
- Think how easy it is for us to go to school up to the age of 16

Postcard 4

- In what ways would your home be the same as the villagers' one? How would it be different?
- What might be the consequences of not having electricity, running water, TV, or a phone?
- Why is it important for the villagers to have God's words written in Manobo?
  So that they can read and understand God's words clearly. The Manobo language means most to them because it is their heart language, the one they learnt first and know best!

For your info...

- The Manobo language has three completely separate dialects. 20,000 people speak each dialect
- There are over 150 languages spoken in the Philippines
- The village has approximately 150 people living in it. They are all related to each other going back two generations

How can we pray for Bible translators?

Use the points highlighted by the postcards and your discussion time. Encourage the children to make personal responses in prayer. For example:

- Thank you God for things we take for granted like having hot baths. Please help missionaries when they are missing them and feel sad and lonely
- Please help bible translators in remote villages to write your words in the language the people know best
- Help them to find the right words when they get stuck
- Give them good friends to check their work for mistakes
- Help them get better and better at the language, so they can talk to the villagers really well and do good translation work

Other ideas

- 'Munch, munch, you're lunch!' game (p 86) — to let the children imagine they are trying to get across the river to the village
- 'How to pray for Asian Christians' and 'How to pray for Asian non-Christians' (p 57-58)
- Make a coconut milk-shake (p 89)

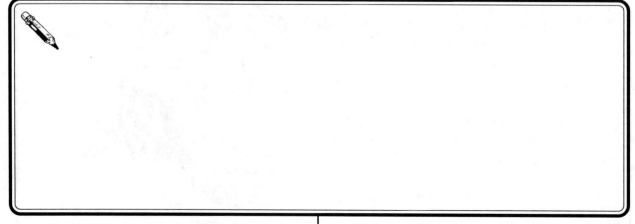

Postcards from the Philippines–2

Postcard 3

Dear St Custards,

The village houses are built of wood and thatch. The church is the same—it has a mud floor, benches to sit on and big gaps in the walls which let air in. About 50 villagers come to worship on Sunday mornings. The small children go to a new nursery school in the village. Everyone speaks Manobo there, but there aren't any school books written in their language. Can you imagine having no books to read? When the children are a bit older, they cross the river to get to primary school. There they have to learn other languages. The 10 year olds in my village can count up to 10 in five different languages! WOW!

Not many children go to secondary school as it's even further away from home. Some young people work in the city, but most stay in the village and help in the rice fields.

From, Roo-Barb

Postcard 4

Dear St Custards,

There's no electricity in my village so everyone goes to bed soon after it gets dark (no one thinks half past eight is an uncool bedtime for a grownup!) But we get up really early at half past five (yawn!) when the sun starts to shine.

First thing in the morning the church is peaceful and I have my quiet time there—reading, praying and listening to God. After breakfast I go to the fields to help the farmers in their work. We chat a lot and I learn new words in Manobo every day. There are no water taps in the village, so while everyone else is resting during the hot time in the afternoon, I go up the river a bit to have my bath—in private! Then I do some thinking (which is hard work) about what to say at the bible study and the service in church. My big job here is to translate the Old Testament stories about God into Manobo. In the evening some friends help me check the stories for spelling mistakes and things like that. I usually do one chapter a week. I'm working on Genesis at the minute, so there's still a lot of work to do!

Those first visitors to the village translated all the New Testament into Manobo—it took 11 years to do! Now that they can read about God in the language that they love most, the Manobo Christians are very happy!

From, Roo-Barb

What's it like?
A radio worker in Thailand – 1

What is it?

The first two links in a chain of events, showing radio's part in evangelism.

What will they learn?

- Christian Radio reaches people in remote areas
- Radio work is an important link in spreading the gospel

What do you do?

Preparation

- Photocopy the sheets

On the day

- Bring in a radio. Let the children tune it in to different stations. Discuss what stations they hear at home. Have they ever heard a Christian radio programme?
- Have different children read each link out loud
- Lead discussions based on the following ideas:

Link 1

Radio is the only way for some people to hear the gospel. To draw this out, ask questions like:

- Why didn't the people where Sunisa lived—her local pastor or Sunday School teacher—tell her about God?
  They didn't know God and there wasn't a pastor or a Sunday School to go to
- When and where did you first hear about God?
  Compare your experience with Sunisa's

Link 2

There are different jobs to do in a radio station, including: maintaining the technical equipment, finding Christians speakers from minority language groups, and replying to letters from listeners. They reply by sending literature, Bible Correspondence Courses and linking people up with groups of believers.

Note: It is more difficult to do this work in a closed country like China.

- If Tom had written a reply to Sunisa's letter, what important things would he tell her about Jesus?

For your info...

- Christian radio stations broadcast in over 210 languages around the world
- There are 1,200 million radio receivers in the world
- Most of the world's population have access to a radio
- A lot of electricity is needed to power for transmitters. Radio waves travel thousands of miles and must not be drowned by other local radio programmes

How can we pray for radio work?

Use the points noted above as a guide for your prayers. People to pray for include:

- The radio technicians, speakers/DJs, producers, script writers, translators, and those who reply to letters
- Radio listeners hearing about Jesus for the first time today
- Those listening to Christian programmes who have a different religion or none at all
- Those living in countries where the gospel is not allowed to be preached or followed, but who hear it on the radio
- That those hearing the message will believe and trust in Jesus

A radio worker in Thailand – 1

Link 1 — Sunisa writes a letter

Sunisa lived in the countryside, miles away from town. She loved listening to the radio. One day she heard a Christian talking about Jesus. The speaker said anyone interested in finding out more about this God could write in to the radio station. So Sunisa got a sheet of paper and carefully wrote her address on it. She politely asked if someone could come to tell her more about Jesus, as no-one in her village knew about this person. She really did want to know but she was only 11 years old. Would her letter be taken seriously or laughed at and tossed in the bin?

Link 2 — DJ Tom

At seven Tom dreamed of becoming a DJ. He thought it would be the coolest job in the whole world! For hours he practised on his special radio voice, saying funny things into a hairbrush microphone like, 'this is DJ Tom, the man with the gift of the gab...' Some years later, Tom studied radio broadcasting at university and then decided to use his talents for God. He began working for a Christian radio station in Thailand.

The station put out on the air programmes about the God he loved and served. Tom was surprised at the number of letters coming in to the station—most were from people living in remote areas who didn't know anyone nearby who was a Christian. One day he got a letter from a young girl. Tom started to pray for her asking God to show him what he could do to help. He got a map of the area and found where the girl was living. There was a red dot on the map a few miles from her village. Tom went to the phone and made a call to the person living there.

What's it like?
A church worker in Thailand – 2

What is it?

Five more links in a chain of events showing the different jobs a church worker does, and the pressures new Christians sometimes face.

What will they learn?

- God can use young people as well as adults to witness to others
- Church work involves visiting, evangelism, preaching, church planting and leadership training

What do you do?

Preparation

- Photocopy the sheet
- Investigate the possibility of having one of your church leaders come to the class

On the day

- Involve the children in planning, conducting and maybe recording an interview with your minister/vicar/pastor. Ask about the different jobs he does in a week
- Have volunteers read each of the remaining links
- Lead discussion based on the following ideas:

Link 3

Ben, the vet, became a church worker

- Are the jobs similar?

Sometimes God asks people to do a completely different job for him!

Link 4

To demonstrate the small number of Christians living in Thailand, name a place 30 miles from where you are. Explain that's how far away the nearest Christian was to Sunisa.

Think of all the people who live between these two places or in a 30 mile radius of your area. Try to imagine none of them ever having heard about God. Use a big map to show the two places.

Link 5

Look at the word 'witness'

- What does it mean?
  A witness is someone who has seen or experienced something and can tell others about it. Christians know Jesus and so we can show or tell others about him
- Are you a witness for God?
  Everyone who knows Jesus is a witness or example of what it means to be a Christian. You are either a good witness or a bad witness
- How did Sunisa witness to her family?
  By believing in God and not turning away from him
- What did Sunisa's family want her to do?
  Turn back to worshipping their god (Buddha)
- What happened as a result of her witness?
  All her family came to know Jesus

Link 6

Ben's churches have Sunday schools. Often the first members of a new church are mums who bring their babies and children to meetings.

- How are Ben's churches different from yours?
  Probably much smaller, buildings, etc...

Link 7

List the different jobs Ben does as a church worker. Compare these with what your pastor does.

- Can you spot any similarities or differences?

For your info...

- Sunisa, her brother and his wife all went to Bible college
- Afterwards, Sunisa worked as a full-time evangelist at a hospital in Thailand
- She is now working in a village

How can we pray for church workers?

- Pray for God's blessing on tiny churches scattered all over Thailand. Pray for the busy pastors spending a lot of time travelling between them
- Pray for young people and grown-ups belonging to these remote churches as they witness to everyone around them
- Pray that their friends, families and neighbours will be curious to find out more about God
- Pray for the leader of each church to do a good job of looking after others
- Pray the churches will get bigger and bigger
- Thank God for the people who were links in a chain to Sunisa's family becoming Christians

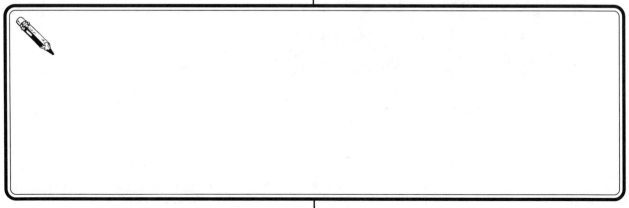

A church worker in Thailand – 2

Link 3 — Ben's lambs

Ben was born on a farm where there were lots of sheep and cows, three dogs and four cats! His special job at home was to look after the sick lambs. Ben made sure they were warm and had lots of milk to drink. He loved taking care of the animals and when he grew up, Ben became a vet. He thought he would be a vet forever, but God had a very different job for him to do next. Ben went to Thailand to be a church worker.

Every morning from Monday to Friday he would hop on his motorbike and set off to do some visiting. Ben had 14 tiny churches to look after spread out in every direction! One day, Ben got a phone call that sent him off to speak with someone who had heard about God by listening to a Christian radio programme.

Link 4 — Sunisa's answer

Some days after Sunisa posted her letter, a person arrived on her doorstep. He had travelled 30 miles on his motorbike to come and tell her about Jesus! Sunisa and the man prayed together and she became a Christian. The man gave her a bible to read. Who was he? Ben of course! And he could hardly wait to tell Tom the good news about Sunisa.

Link 5 — Sunisa's witness

Being a Christian at home was hard for Sunisa. Her family did not like her worshipping a strange god. Her dad got so angry he beat her. He even tried to burn her bible, but it wouldn't light! One night, while Sunisa was sleeping, her mosquito net caught fire. Flames were all around her but she was kept safe. Sunisa's family realised that her God was keeping her safe. After that her dad and mum, uncles and aunts and sister and brother all believed in Jesus.

Link 6 — The 15th church

Sunisa's house is built on stilts. The coolest place to sit is underneath in the shade! On Sundays the whole family meet there to worship God together. Now Ben has another little church to care for—that's number 15! How had the others started? Each began with only one or two people in it. When Ben visits his church members, he often meets their families, friends and neighbours as well. Sometimes they are very curious about God and ask Ben to explain things to them too. This is how the tiny churches first start, and then get a little bigger.

Link 7 — Sunisa's brother

Ben is teaching one person from each church how to take care of it. He wants them to do the work when he's not there. If Ben is busy visiting one of the other churches, then Sunisa's brother is in charge. Ben has taught him how to preach and lead Bible studies and lots of other things too.

What's it like?
A medical missionary – 1

What is it?

A day in the life of a missionary doctor, seen from the eyes of a passing gecko!

What will they learn?

- What it means to work as a doctor in a mission hospital
- To turn to Jesus now rather than wait until the last chance
- That we should all be involved in helping others and not think of ourselves more highly than we ought

What do you do?

Preparation

- Make photocopies of the story for the children to colour in

On the day

- Let different children read the story out loud
- Lead discussion based on the following ideas:

Ward 1:

- What did the sick lady do first when she found out she was ill?
  Wore charms, followed superstition
- What did she try next?
  Witch doctor, magic
- When did she go to the Christian hospital?
  When it was almost too late
- When you're in trouble or something has gone wrong, how do you try to fix things?
  Try and fix them yourself, go your own way, don't turn to God
- When should we ask God for help?
  Right away!

Don't turn to God at the last chance.

Ward 2:

- Why did the local doctors not want to help?
  Lazy, too proud
- Was Dr Broto proud? What did he do when he found out what was wrong?
  Prayed and acted quickly
- What do you do when someone at school or home needs help?
- Do you help even if you think it's not your job? That someone else should be doing it?
- Jesus set us an example by not being proud. He helped all sorts of people and did the jobs no one else would stoop to. He told us to serve each other, not to expect people to serve us. If we act like him, what do you think people will say?
  different lifestyle, how can I find out more

How can we pray for medical missionaries?

- Pray for strength for missionary doctors. They often have to work long hours in the heat. And if there are no other hospitals nearby, they have to be able to cope with anything
- Pray for safety. The bugs and germs missionary doctors have to deal with are often different from the ones they knew at home. Travel on the roads can also be dangerous
- Usually all the doctors live near each other on the hospital compound. Pray that they would get on well with each other. This can be difficult when they're tired or need a break
- Pray that doctors and nurses would have enough time to read their Bibles and pray regularly. Pray that they would walk closely with Jesus
- Pray for more Christian doctors and nurses to leave their homes and work in countries where Jesus isn't known
- Pray for the training of local Christian doctors and nurses who can take over the work of the hospital from the missionaries

Other ideas

- 'Gecko maina' (p 63) — find out what being a gecko is all about
- 'How to pray...' (pp 55-58) — pray for a medical missionary you know
- Sing in Indonesian (p 76)

Guy the Medical Gecko – 1

Hi! I'm Guy the Gecko, and I live in a Christian hospital in Indonesia. Let me show you around.

Sorry if these pictures are from a funny angle, but I walk on the ceiling to catch flies!

Ward 1

You'll have to be very quiet in this room, because there's a very sick lady here. She'd been sick for weeks, and kept getting worse. But she didn't come to the Christian hospital, even though she knew it was good at healing people.

The first thing she tried was to wear some charms. She tied some beads and bracelets around her wrists that were supposed to be magic. But she kept getting worse.

Next she went to the witch doctor. He asked for lots of money for payment. He sacrificed some chickens and did some other secret magic things. It didn't work. She went back to the witch doctor and spent all she had on smelly potions, trying to get better. But she kept getting worse.

When she ran out of money, the witch doctor wouldn't see her again. Her family gave up hope and thought she'd die. They brought her to the Christian hospital as a last chance. It was almost too late.

The hospital didn't ask for money first. They gave her medicines to make her better. But it would have been best if she had come to the hospital straight away.

Can you see someone under the bed? Until she gets well, someone from the sick lady's family will sleep under the bed and cook her food.

Ward 2

You can make as much noise as you like in this room—I can't hear anything above the baby's crying!

Mummies don't usually come in to the hospital to have their babies. But this time things were going wrong. The baby just didn't want to come out! So the baby's older brother ran miles and miles to get to the hospital. He knew his mummy needed help, but it was late last night when he arrived. Most of the local doctors were in bed, and they didn't want to get up. And anyway, they said, driving an ambulance is not a job for a *doctor!*

But when Dr Broto heard the boy's story, he prayed for help, jumped into his car, and drove over the lanes and fields to get to the village. He bundled the mummy into the car and raced back. She almost gave birth on the way!

This morning, the baby was born safely. The mummy is so happy, she has decided to call the baby 'Toyota', named after the doctor's car that came to get her! She also wants to find out why he was so kind to her.

What's it like?
A medical missionary – 2

What is it?

A day in the life of a missionary doctor, seen from the eyes of a passing gecko!

What will they learn?

- What it means to work as a doctor in a mission hospital
- How doctors work as a team and try to share the gospel as well as heal the sick
- That we should pray about the big things and the small things

What do you do?

Preparation

- Make photocopies of the story for the children to colour in

On the day

- Let different children read the story out loud
- Lead discussion based on the following ideas:

Operating Theatre

- Why is it so clean in the Operating Theatre?
  To keep germs out
- Why do the doctors do their best?
  They want to heal their patients. And it shows others who aren't yet Christans that they do their best because they love Jesus
- If you do your best for Jesus, other people might sit up and notice!
- When do the doctors pray for the patient?
  Before they start, if things are easy and if things get hard
- God is interested in the big things as well as the small things. What do you pray about? When do you pray?
  You can pray about anything at any time. God is interested in you

Out Patients Department

- What are the doctors doing? Why don't they have time to talk to the patients?
  Seeing patients, trying to give good medical advice, too many to spend much time with each
- What does Mr Susilo and his friends do while people are waiting?
  Talks about Jesus, explains the gospel, talks to the big group and with individuals
- Have you ever tried to do everything yourself? Is it possible?
- The doctors can't do everything! They can't always talk about Jesus as well as give out medicine. That's why they work as part of a team. Do you work well with other people?
- What happens to some people when they understand about Jesus?
  They believe in him and become Christians
- What might happen when the new Christians go home?
  Their friends and family believe too, start a new church. Also pressure to give up their new faith

How can we pray for medical missionaries?

- Pray that doctors and nurses would have wisdom and skill. Because there's no one else to do the job, they are often thrown in at the deep end and have to do jobs they've not been trained for
- Sometimes it can be lonely, especially when a doctor has to make a difficult decision, and there's no other specialist doctors to ask for advice
- Pray that patients, nurses and people living locally will become Christians. Pray that the hospitals and doctors would not just be healing the outsides of people, but the God would be healing their insides and drawing them to know and love Jesus
- Pray for people who have become Christians and are returning to their homes. They will need Christian friends if they are to grow in their new faith. Pray that new churches would start because of the work of Christian doctors and nurses

Other ideas

- 'Gecko maina' (p 63) — find out what being a gecko is all about
- 'How to pray for Asian Christians and non-Christians' (pp 57-58)
- Sing in Indonesian (p 76)

Guy the Medical Gecko – 2

Operating Theatre

Here we are in the Operating Theatre. I need to make myself very small because if a nurse finds me, I'll get walloped. They keep this room very clean—everyone has to wear a gown and a mask, and I haven't got one!

Most of the nurses here aren't Christians. They work at this hospital because they know they will get good training. They also know the doctors and the Christian nurses care for people, and try to do the best job they can. It's the best hospital in the area!

Before they get to work, the doctors always pray. Even if it's an easy operation, they ask God for help. They also ask God to show the patients how much he loves them, and that the patient would come to know him as their friend.

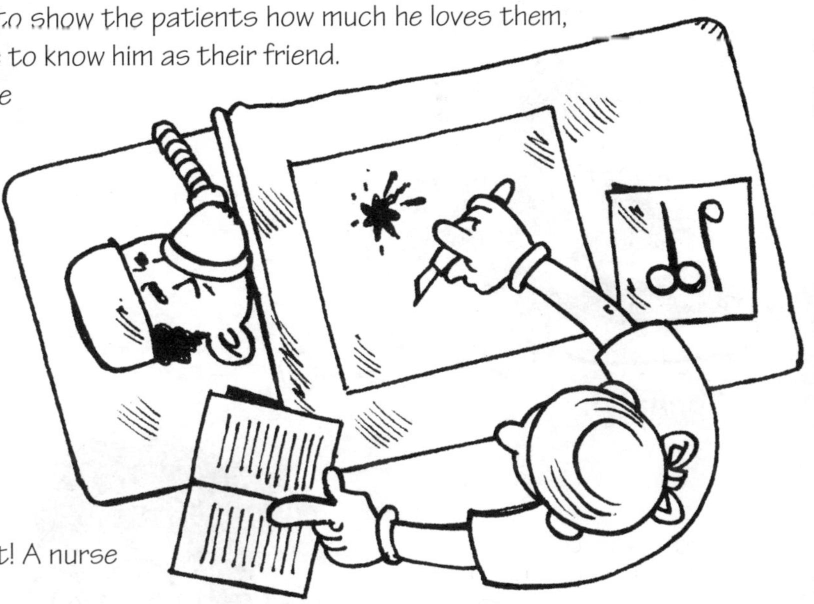

If something goes wrong in the operation, or if things are hard, the doctors pray again. Sometimes they have to do operations that are new to them. Today a friend of Dr Broto's is holding open a text book as they try to save the patient's life.

Ooooh! I'm feeling a bit woozy from the sight of blood. I hope I don't faint and fall onto the operating table! Yeowch! Look out! A nurse has spotted me. I'd better run!

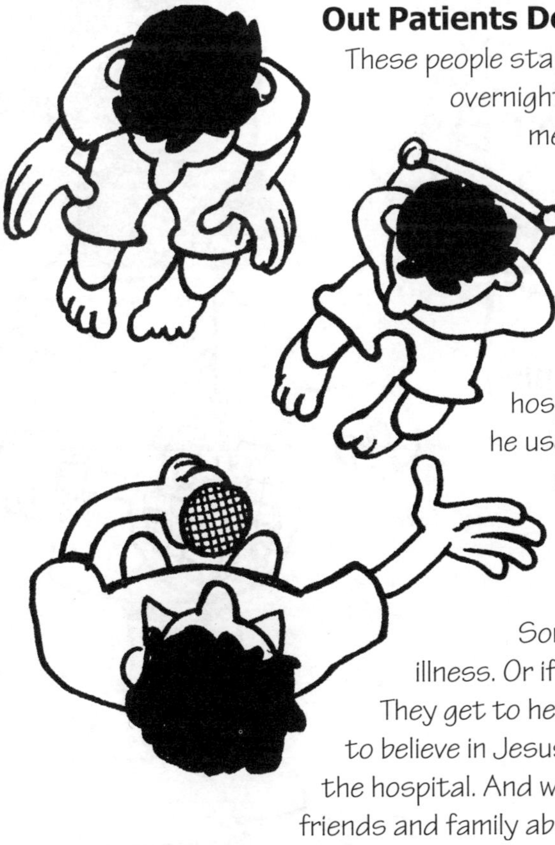

Out Patients Department

These people start queueing long before breakfast! They don't stay overnight, but come to the hospital to see a doctor or pick up medicine. The doctors work very hard trying to see as many people as they can. They don't have much time to talk with the patients. But if there are lots of people, some may have to wait for hours. While they're waiting, Mr Susilo talks to them. He's from a nearby city, and he speaks Indonesian. You can see him holding the microphone. He is the hospital evangelist and he tells them about God. Often he uses pictures on a big board so that the patients can understand what he's talking about. Then he and some of his helpers will go and sit with people, talking to them. Some of them are interested in Jesus because they've never heard of him before.

Some people come back day after day because of their illness. Or if they're in bed, Mr Susilo will come and visit them. They get to hear more and more about Jesus. A few of them come to believe in Jesus and love him. That's how the church started near the hospital. And when people who have been sick go home, they tell their friends and family about Jesus, and the good news spreads.

Kids like me!

Donnalyn

Hashimoto

Wang Li Bing

Onka-Shooey

Daow

Kids like me

Contents

How to use this section

What is it?

A series of handouts to show children what their lives would be like if they'd been born in another country.

What do you need?

- Coloured pens/pencils etc for colouring in

What do you do?

Preparation

- Photocopy the worksheets. They fit on two sides of A4 except 'Daow'

On the day

- Hand out photocopies
- Let children read them at their own pace
- Provide coloured pens/pencils for them to colour the pictures in

You may wish to follow up with...

- Discussion about how they might feel if they had been born in the country they have read about
- Prayer for kids in the country they have read about. Encourage them to draw from what they have just learnt. Prayers could be written by individuals or might be spoken spontaneously

Other ideas

You may want to use the 'Kids like me' poster on p 42 as publicity before the meeting, or to show the children who else they'll meet in future classes. Enlarge it on a photocopier to A3 and colour in.

These can also be useful 'filler' items to keep up your sleeve. Have a few copies available for children who finish other activities early.

Hashimoto – Japan

Hisayoshi Hashimoto is 11 years old. He lives near the city of Kobe in Japan.

Hashimoto's mum is a maths teacher and his dad a company director. Both work very hard so Hashimoto has to help with the housework . . . that is, when he's not watching his favourite tv programme, Mr Bean, or playing baseball with his best friend, Shimotani.

One morning at 5.46 am (early or what!?) he was sitting at his desk swotting over his lessons for that day. All of a sudden an earthquake struck and his house just collapsed into rubble. It was scary biscuits for his whole family. Amazingly they escaped with only a few scratches and bruises.

Hashimoto now lives in a temporary house with his mum, dad, four brothers, two hamsters and three cats. At first when he brought his hamsters home he was worried the cats might gobble them up for breakfast. Instead they thought the hamsters were their babies and produced milk for them!

His favourite food is rice balls with seaweed and pickled plum. His family eat rice and fish for at least one meal a day.

To count to five Hashimoto says...
1 ichi
2 ni
3 san
4 shi
5 go

His favourite comics are about dinosaurs and he's seen Jurassic Park loads of times now.

There's nothing Hashimoto likes more than jumping into a very hot bath and lying in it up to his neck for as long as he can. It's a kind of Japanese endurance test, laughs Hashimoto, but he says it's good for his patience! He enjoys the bath most in the Japanese winters when there's heavy snow on the ground and its (brrr!) freezing outside. In winter he sleeps on a mattress (called a futon) on a wooden floor with special heating.

His best subject is maths but he says he's not as clever as his three big brothers. They all went to the No.1 High school in Japan. Hashimoto is worried he won't make it and his parents will be very disappointed. They gave him the name 'Hashimoto' meaning 'great' and 'good' but he's not sure he can live up to it.

Hashimoto goes to school six days a week. He can't wait until next year when he won't have to wear a school uniform.

His family are atheists. They just don't believe in God at all. Hashimoto has never been to church. He has never heard a thing about Jesus ... but when he dies he thinks he will meet God.

He always dreads art class but loves break time when he does muscle training with his friends.

When he grows up he wants to be a famous doctor and operate on people all over the world ... as well as marry a girl who can make the best rice balls in Japan! Right now he likes being young because when you grow up in Japan you're not allowed to make mistakes.

Wang Li Bing – China

His mum and dad are both factory workers at the No. 2 Shanghai Cotton Mill. Wang Li Bing's grandmother does most of the cooking. She uses a big pan called a wok and most days they eat rice or noodles with meat and vegetables. His grandmother is famous for her homemade dumplings stuffed with meat, onions, garlic and ginger. What Wang Li Bing really enjoys is sucking on a delicious juicy chicken's claw covered with chilli sauce.

Wang Li Bing thinks his hardest subject is Chinese. This is how he writes his name. 王力兵 Instead of 26 letters in the alphabet they have 50,000 characters to learn. He has to learn about 5,000 at primary school!

His favourite clothes are his track suit even though it's also his school uniform. In winter he wears a jumper and woolly trousers underneath. Sometimes when it gets really cold he has five layers on! Wang Li Bing prefers the summer time, when you can buy watermelons in Shanghai. One the size of your head costs only 1 yuan (10p!)

Kids like me

Wang Li Bing lives in an apartment block in Shanghai. He lives with his mother 'mama', father 'baba', grandmother, grandfather and two goldfish. He has no brothers or sisters. Families in China are only allowed one child because there are already over one billion people. The government is worried there won't be enough food to go round.

Wang Li Bing likes reading comics by himself and he loves anything about kung fu or Bruce Lee. He also watches lots of tv especially foreign cartoons. He says Chinese tv is boring.

They have two rooms and a small kitchen. Wang Li Bing sleeps in his parent's room. They have to share a bathroom with other families on their floor.

Wang Li Bing's best friend is Pang Ai Ming. Both are mad about flying kites and stamp collecting! They've stopped playing together after school though as Pang Ai Ming has to stay late for his exercise class. His aunties spoiled him with so many sweet cakes that he's grown very, very, chubby. If he doesn't pass his PE exam he won't be able to enter a key middle school (one of the top ones).

His most fantastic dream is one day to fly to the stars in a Chinese spaceship!

Wang Li Bing catches a lift to school on the back of his dad's bicycle . . . or sits on the crossbar if his mum is on the back. Only important officials in China have cars.

When he grows up Wang Li Bing would like to be a businessman, wear a suit and make lots of money. He would like to marry a beautiful girl but thinks she would only marry him if he was rich. Anyway, he'd still rather be young because you have more time to play than grown-ups.

This year Wang Li Bing went to a summer school run by young teachers from the UK. They were very kind and never lost their tempers. They taught his class lots of funny games and songs. His grandmother thinks they are Christians. Wang Li Bing laughed so much this summer English is now his favourite subject!

At break time he plays table tennis or pretends to sing karaoke with his friends.

School is six days a week and begins with exercises in the courtyard at 7.45 am. After that everyone salutes the Chinese flag.

Wang Li Bing's parents are atheists and don't believe in God at all. He would like to read the Bible and go to church but in China no-one under 18 is allowed to. In politics class the teacher told him there is no great God, only the Chinese people are great. Wang Li Bing only feels naughty and lazy inside. Maybe his teacher is wrong and there is a heaven. Before he dies he'd definitely like to find out something about Jesus.

Donnalyn – the Philippines

Donnalyn is eight years old. She lives in Manila, the capital city of the Philippines, with her mum ('nanay'), her dad ('tatay'), her brother and sister and their dog called Yoco.

Her little sister, Lollipop, is four years old and her brother, Immanuel is only two.

They all live together in one big room in a wooden building. One corner of the room is the 'sala' area where they sit. There is a shelf for the tv , a shelf for the kitchen and a bed. Next to the bed is a table and three chairs. At mealtimes some of the family have to sit on the bed.

Donnalyn's best friend is Kathleen. She likes her because she is very funny. They go rollerblading together and sometimes play Jacks and dodge ball.

The family have electricity so they can have a fridge, but there is no running water to their house. They have to go to the tap downstairs when they need to wash.

Donnalyn helps her mum and dad with the housework. She sweeps the floor and sometimes baby sits Lollipop and Immanuel.

Donnalyn's dad works as a labourer in his sister's company. They make soft furnishings and he helps pack and deliver goods. They are busy at the moment so he is working every day.

Rice is her family's main food although sometimes they eat bread for breakfast. They usually eat vegetables with it and fish or meat on a special occasion.

Donnalyn's favourite food is fried chicken, rice and sinigang with ketchup. Sinigang is made from a green leafy vegetable called kangkong. Donnalyn loves ketchup but Lollipop won't eat it at all. She thinks it looks like blood!

Donnalyn can't imagine what it would be like to have her own room. Her whole family (apart from Yoco!) sleep together on the one double bed. It has a mattress and they usually only need a sheet on top.

Donnalyn goes to school five days a week. Her school is called the United Methodist Christian School She wears a white shirt with the school logo sewn on and a navy blue skirt.
She carries her books in a red school bag on wheels, like a little shopping trolley.

Donnalyn usually wears a sleeveless top and shorts and likes to kick her shoes off whenever she can.

She hardly ever wears a long-sleeved shirt because it never really gets cold in winter.

She likes wearing her PE uniform best of all. It is a white t-shirt and navy shorts.

When Donnalyn grows up she would like to be a teacher. When she comes home from school she often plays schools. She is the teacher and Lollipop and Immanuel are the pupils.

She likes all her subjects at school but her favourite is GMRC (Good Morals and Right Conduct).

Donnalyn and her classmates don't have space to play outside so they take their break times in the classroom.

Donnalyn's family are Christians and they go to the Door of Hope Christian Fellowship. It is in the wooden building where they live so she only has to go down her steps to get to church!

Donnalyn learns a lot of things about Jesus at the church. She knows He loves her and He died for her.
She says of all the things she ever dreams of doing the best is to see Jesus some day.

She would also like to visit Canada because pastor Frank, her missionary friend lives there now.

When she is grown-up she would like to marry a man who is kind and handsome and a Christian.

Right now she likes being young because it's nice to be submissive and she likes following her elders.

Onka-Shooey — Indonesia

Onka-Shooey lives in a house on a six lane highway in Jakarta, the capital city of Indonesia. He is eight years old and this is the fifth house he has lived in. He lives with his mum and dad and his two big brothers. There are always lots of traffic jams on their street. Sometimes after playing outside Onka-Shooey gets grit in his teeth and black dust up his nose from the pollution.

His dad lectures in a university on how to teach the Bible. His mum looks after them all at home. When Onka-Shooey and his brothers were small she had more than 100 nappies a week to wash and no washing machine!

Onka-Shooey and his family are Scottish. He has only been to Scotland once and can hardly remember what baked beans taste like or what a double-decker bus is!

They have two rabbits called Itchy and Scratchy. At the market you can buy all kinds of animals like squirrels and baby owls and snakes but Onka-Shooey's mum says there's no room for any more pets. Onka-Shooey shares a room with his brothers. They have bunk beds and one single bed with really big springs. Until they were found out they used to do dive bombs onto the single bed from the top bunk!

Every morning Onka-Shooey has rice porridge for breakfast. Sometimes for a special treat, like on his birthday, he has cornflakes. In Indonesia the milk is made up from powder. His biggest brother says that in Scotland you get milk from a cow, and it's already watered. His favourite food is corn on the cob, soaked in a sugary-chilli sauce, and barbecued over a charcoal fire.

Onka-Shooey likes to run around barefoot because shoes are too hot and sweaty. The only problem is the red ants nip his toes. Once he stood on a rusty nail and had to have it bandaged. He stayed in his mum and dad's bed all day, sipping Sprite and reading Jungle Book.

Onka-Shooey goes away to school in Malaysia, which means two plane journeys and a four hour taxi ride. He has two terms a year, each for four months. He always brings presents back from school for his mum and dad. Last time he got them facecloths with 'British Airways' written on them.

He spends the long school holidays at home with his family. Sometimes they all go on adventures together. Onka-Shooey has climbed volcanoes and boiled eggs in the hot pools at the top. They taste a bit pongy! They also go to the beach and swim in lagoons, hack through the jungle, and fish for sea snakes.

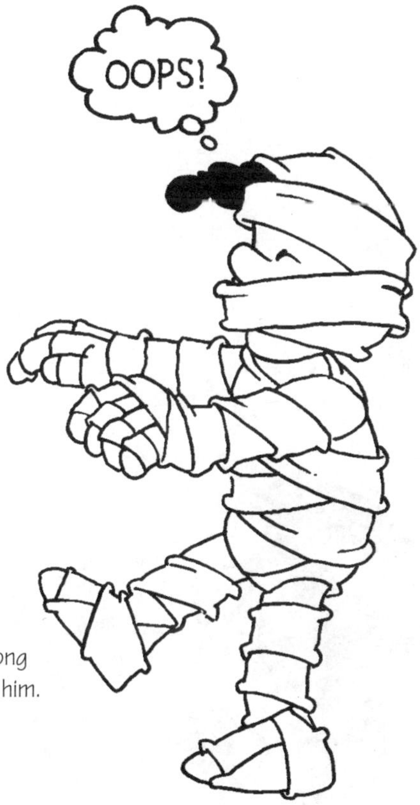

His favourite clothes are shorts and a t-shirt. At night he wears a sarong in bed. This is a big piece of cloth sewn up like a tube and wrapped round him. All men in Indonesia wear them. They are nice and cool.

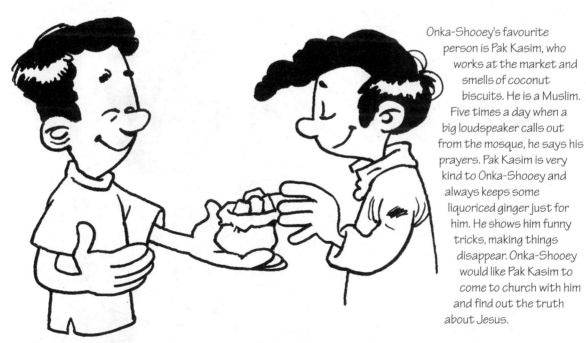

Onka-Shooey's favourite person is Pak Kasim, who works at the market and smells of coconut biscuits. He is a Muslim. Five times a day when a big loudspeaker calls out from the mosque, he says his prayers. Pak Kasim is very kind to Onka-Shooey and always keeps some liquoriced ginger just for him. He shows him funny tricks, making things disappear. Onka-Shooey would like Pak Kasim to come to church with him and find out the truth about Jesus.

When Onka-Shooey grows up he wants to be an engineer and a missionary. There are some far away Indonesian islands where no missionary has ever gone. Pak Kasim says he's heard they eat people there! Maybe Onka-Shooey will just be an engineer!

Onka-Shooey says when he dies, he will wake up in Jesus' home and never have to move house again. That will be heaven!

Daow — Thailand

Everyone who knows Mayuree Tongpoon calls her 'Daow,' which means 'turtle.' She's 12 years old and lives in a small village called Klong Wan by the sea in South Thailand.

In Thailand everyone has a nickname and they hardly use their real names. One of Daow's friend's has a nickname meaning 'Elephant'!

Daow wears t-shirts and shorts most of the time. In Thailand it is not polite to wear shoes inside so she likes to wear shoes that are easy to kick off.

Daow lives with her mum and dad. Their family shop is at the front of the house. They sell clocks and watches, so she has no excuse for being late for school. Daow has to help in the shop in the evenings. In Thailand the shops stay open until ten o'clock at night because it is so warm outside.

On the way home from school Daow and her friends like to buy a yummy snack from the village market. Their favourite is sticky rice sold in a hollowed out bamboo stick. On really hot days they buy ice-cream or lollies, but you have to eat them quickly because they melt so fast!

Daow is happiest when she is with her friends from school. Every night they play badminton together in the grounds of the temple in Klong Wan. They have a mini-league and are really proud of their friend 'Egg' who has just won a big badminton competition in the nearest big town.

Daow and her family are Buddhists. They think the Buddhist religion is an important part of being Thai. When her brother Karoen was 12 years old he became a Buddhist monk for one week. He lived in the temple with the other monks and wore bright orange robes.

When Daow grows up she would like to work in a hotel in a big city like Bangkok.

Very early in the morning the Buddhist monks walk around Klong Wan collecting 'alms' (gifts of food or money). There isn't a church in Klong Wan and Daow doesn't have any friends who love Jesus.

At the weekend they play on the beach watching the fishermen come in with their nets. Daow's favourite boat is a bright red and blue one. Sometimes the owner lets her have a fish to take home.

Support

Contents

How to use this section

What is it?

Handouts giving practical tips on how to support your missionary and Asian Christians. The following notes refer to the 'How to pray...' worksheets

What do you need?

- Coloured pens/pencils etc for colouring in

What do you do?

Preparation

- Photocopy the worksheets

On the day

- Hand out the photocopies
- Let the children read them through at their own pace, or let different children read out individual paragraphs
- Let them colour in the pictures
- You may wish to lead discussion on some of the topics so that you are sure the children understand them
- Ask the children for prayer points they want to use. If you know missionaries, MKs or people in Asia, pray for them by name
- Encourage the children to take the worksheets home and to pray on their own or with their parents during the rest of the week

Praying together

- Depending on the group, it may be best if you simply pray on your own at the end
- You can lead prayer by praying in phrases, and have the children repeat after you
- Ask individual children to pick out one paragraph from the worksheet and pray for those things
- Always praise children who are learning to pray!

Send a care package

What is it?

To get the children practically involved in making, wrapping and sending a care package to a missionary or mission family overseas.

Why?

In the early church, Christians looked after each other. We can support our missionaries by sending them a package to show that we care about them.
See: Acts 11:27-30; Rom 15:26; 2 Cor 8:1-4.

What do you do?

There are lots of ideas for what you can send in a care package. The more you know about your missionaries, the easier it is for you to know what would be appropriate and appreciated by them.

General guidelines

- Use bubble wrap or padded envelopes for extra protection.
- Keep packages small, well secured and labelled, with a return address on the back.
- Do not send breakable, heavy or perishable items in the post.
- Do not send rice to Asia!
- Do not put perfumed goods (eg soap, talc) in the same packet as eatable goods.

Ideas

- **Photos**
  Take a photo of your group and get everyone to sign it or let each child bring in a small photo of themselves to send.
- **Cards**
  Make birthday (or christmas) cards for each member of the family—write on the envelopes who it is for and when it can be opened.
- **Letters**
  Get each child to write about themselves—their family, school, what games they play and other activities, their holidays, favourite books, toys and films or videos, pets etc...They could ask the missionary kids any questions they can think of.
- **Tapes**
  Make a tape (cassette or video!), with each child briefly interviewed—include favourite jokes and the group singing.
- **Gifts**
  Invite each child to bring in a small gift (less than £1.00) for a missionary kid. Here are some suggestions to get you thinking:
  - pencil, pen, rubber, ruler, sharpener, magic invisible marker, rubber stamp and pad, crayons, felt tips, plastic toys—water pistol, robot, car, lego kit, bouncey ball, comics, colourful writing paper, poster, stickers, puzzles.
- **Food**
  A bag of pick'n'mix sweets, mini chocolate bar treats, chewing gum (crisps don't travel well!)
- **For the adults**
  Local newspapers/interesting articles cut out or magazines are also welcome. Is there a favourite food they cannot get in their country?

To involve the children as much as possible during the process, let them wrap up their gifts in class and put in personal notes.

Report back next week, telling them the weight of the parcel and how much it cost to send plus how long it will take to get there.

Show on the world map exactly where the parcel is going. Whenever a reply comes back from the missionary, read this out to the children.

What to say:

- What things does the postman deliver to your house? *cards, letters, parcels...*
- What kinds of cards do you get? *(Birthday, Christmas, Valentine's Day cards, postcards...)*
- Its very exciting getting a surprise in the post. Missionaries love to hear from people at home and to get surprises!

How to pray for new missionaries

Pray for missionaries who've just left their family and friends. Pray that they won't feel too homesick. Ask God to help them when they can't speak the language yet to be friendly and kind, so that people know that they want to be friends with them.

Pray for someone who will help with learning the language. Pray that this friend won't be afraid to show the missionary when he's made a mistake, either in what he's saying or doing.

Pray for a special friend who will help the new missionary to read the street signs, be able to count the money, to know what kind of food to buy, and how to go shopping.

Pray that they will get used to people staring at them, or calling out, 'Hello Mister!' (even if they're women!) Help them to be patient if people pinch their children's cheeks, and to understand that they are just being affectionate in their different way of showing it.

Pray that the missionary will *listen* well to the way the language teacher speaks. Pray that he won't be afraid of making mistakes or get upset if people laugh at him, but that he'll be able to laugh along with them.

Remember that missionaries are like people in glass houses—they don't have much privacy. People like watching them, because they're different. So pray that the missionary will get used to being watched. And pray that he won't behave in a way that puts the people off. Pray that he'll live in a way that attracts people to Jesus.

How to pray for 'Missionary Kids' (MKs)

Pray for missionary families during holiday time, that the days and weeks they have together will be very special. That they'll be able to talk about any worries or fears, or experiences that have upset them. Pray that they'll have really good fun and family times that they can remember later on.

Pray that God will help both parents and children as they write to each other, that their letters won't give a wrong picture, but will help parents to get a picture of what the children are doing. And for the children to understand the kind of work the parents are doing. Pray that letters will bring happiness to those who get them. Pray they won't go astray in the post and get lost!

Remember the children who are leaving home for the first time. That they'll get over homesickness and make friends quickly. You know how important a good friend is at school. Pray that MKs will have special friends who can be a help to them when they're far from home.

Support

Pray for all the members of the family when it's time to say goodbye. Pray for safety on journeys back to school by plane, train, bus, taxi. And pray that none of their luggage will go missing.

With their special understanding of what it feels like to be in another country, MKs are often good at making friends with foreigners who come to the schools and colleges in our country. Pray that they'll be able to tell these friends about the Good News of Jesus.

Older MKs

At some time or other MKs come back to the UK, either for a short time, or to stay. This isn't easy for them, because they don't know the country their parents call 'home.' They are more at home in Asia! They may come from a small Mission school where they know everyone, and the teachers are Christians, and are their friends. They may have to go to a big school in this country where they don't know anybody. They aren't used to people shouting and swearing, and everything is different. Pray that someone will make friends with them and help them adjust to all that is so new.

Pray that MKs will find churches where they feel at home, and people who will understand all the adjustments they're going through.

A lot of MKs go back to their 'home' country in Asia when they're older. Pray that God will use some of them to serve Him as missionaries too.

How to pray for Asian Christians

Pray for Asians who've just become Christians. It's sometimes very hard for them to tell their family the news. The family will find it hard to understand why they've left their old religion. Or they may think of Christianity as a Western religion. Or it may seem they don't love their country. For instance, to be Thai is to be Buddhist. Why join a religion that belongs to the *farangs*, the foreigners?

It is also hard for Christians at certain times of year. During the Muslim Fast Month, at special festivals, or days when the family honours the ancestors or makes offerings to them. Their parents and family may accuse them of not really loving them if they don't join in the celebrations. Ask God to help them specially to know what to do and say. Pray that they will have other Christians at times like this, who can support them and pray with them and help them. Pray they won't get discouraged and give up.

Pray for Christians when they get ill, or their children or parents get ill. Their family or friends may try to persuade them to make an offering, or go to the witch doctor. Pray that they won't go back to the old ways. Pray that even if God doesn't heal the sick person, the Christians won't stop trusting Him.

Ask God to make it possible for Asian pastors and church leaders to get good Bible training, so that they can teach Christians to know God in the right way.

Pray that those who have become Christians will really live differently and be a good witness for Jesus. Pray that they'll be kind and help others; that they will show that they trust God, even when things are hard, or they're very poor. Pray they won't be afraid to tell people about Jesus.

Pray that non-Christians will see that Christians are different—that they know their sins are forgiven; that they have peace; that their lives have really changed. Pray that their friends will want to hear about Jesus too.

How to pray for Asian non-Christians

In some countries, missionaries aren't allowed to go and preach to the people. Let's pray that when people from these countries travel abroad, they will meet up with friendly Christians who will be kind to them, and tell them how much God cares for them.

Pray that Christians won't be afraid to speak to their neighbours about God, and show kindness to them, especially when the neighbours are sick or in trouble.

Some Christian organisations produce radio programmes for countries where the Gospel can't be preached, and where missionaries aren't allowed to go. Pray that people will learn about Jesus by listening to the radio.

It sometimes takes a long time for people to become Christians, because they've been taught another religion, and so they have a lot to un-learn. Or else they've been told that there is no God, or that Christianity is wrong. Ask God to give patience to the pastors and teachers who are trying to help them. And ask God that he will help us to keep praying and not give up!

Let's pray that God will send more missionaries from our countries in the West, and also from Asian churches, so that more people will have the opportunity to hear the Good News about God's Son who loves them.

Most people these days—especially in Asia—want to learn English. Pray for Christians who give English lessons, or teach the Bible in English, that they'll teach clearly and well. And ask God to help many people to find Jesus that way.

In other places, there are very few churches, and not much of a chance for people to hear about Jesus. Pray for churches at Christmas and Easter, that they'll make the best use of the time when people are curious to know the meaning of the celebrations.

Crafts and activities

Contents

'Your passport, please.'

What is it?

A pattern for an international passport. You can put a different stamp in each time you 'visit' a country in your children's programme.

What do you need?

- Passport pattern for each child
- Pens or pencils
- A photo of each child
- Scissors
- Pritt stick
- Height chart
- \+ Date stamp and ink pad
- \+ Other novelty rubber stamps

What do you do?

Preparation

- Ask each child to bring a photo of themselves to this session
- Copy the passport pattern for each child (remember to photocopy at 105% to avoid the spine etc)

On the day

- Hand out copies of the passport pattern
- Help children fill in their details
- Cut photos to fit the space on the passport and glue on
- Every time you visit a different country in your children's programme stamp each passport
- Write the country's name on the official stamp space and stamp the date over it
- Use novelty stamps to add a symbol for each country (eg sun for Japan)

What to say?

In real life, you can't travel to another international country without a passport. On entering through Immigration, the official will say 'Your passport, please'. It will be checked and stamped. Without a passport you are stuck!

Where on earth...?

What is it?

A worksheet for children to do at home, where they record facts about a country in Asia.

What do you need?

- Photocopies of the worksheet (p 95)

What do you do?

Preparation

- Photocopy the worksheet on p 95 (one sheet per child)

The week before

- Give each child a copy of the worksheet
- Decide which country they will research
- If you want each child to look at a different country, write the country name onto their worksheet
- Brainstorm for ideas of where they might find information (eg encyclopedia, parents, school books, library, computer CDs or the web)
- Encourage use of colour so worksheets can be displayed
- Be enthusiastic about next week's session!

On the day

- Praise each child for their efforts
- Invite feedback from the children. Keep your answers until the end
- Use the children's prayer points
- Display the finished worksheets around the room

Other ideas

- Use the 'How to pray...' worksheets (p 55-58)
- Do this exercise regularly so children build up a collection, or until you've papered your room!

Name

SEMI-OFFICIAL PASSPORT

Church

Place official stamps here:

Place photo here:

Name: ______________________________

Address: ______________________________

____

Date of Birth: ____________ Age: ____________

Hair colour: ____________ Eye colour: ____________

Nationality: ____________ Height: ____________

Signature: ______________________________

Gecko mania 1

What is it?

An independent activity page.

Why?

To show that small people can make a big difference.

What do you need?

- Photocopies of activity sheet (p 64)
- Coloured pens or pencils

What to do

Preparation

- Photocopy activity worksheets

On the day

- Give each child an activity sheet/gecko story. Let them read it at their own pace, and colour in the pictures
- Emphasise size doesn't matter! Small people can still make a big difference by prayer

Other ideas

- Use one of the 'How to pray' teaching sessions (pp 55-58) and then pray with the children
- Also do the 'Gecko Mania 2' craft on this page

Gecko mania 2

What is it?

Make your own pet gecko.

Why?

- People come in all sorts of different shapes, sizes and colours, and so do geckos
- Use with 'Gecko Mania 1' on this page

What do you need?

- Photocopies of gecko shapes
- Scissors
- Glue
- Paint, crayons, pencils, or felt tips
- Glitter/glitter glue, tinfoil

+ buttons, beads (for eyes)
+ felt and scraps of material
+ blu-tack (to stick finished geckos to the wall)

What to do

Preparation

- Photocopy gecko shapes on p 65. Enlarge/reduce as required
- ***Either*** make a number of cardboard stencils, **or** give one photocopied sheet to each child

On the day

- Hand out photocopies or let the children draw around the stencils
- Colour and decorate
- Stick on eyes, felt etc
- Cut out and display

What to say

Talk about pets they have, would like to have, and about wild animals. Many children in Asia like to play with geckos.

Show real photos or pictures of lizards, crocodiles and geckos from library books on animals. Geckos are not dangerous wild animals, but they do not need people to look after them. Geckos are very useful because they eat flies and mosquitos that carry diseases.

- See 'Gecko Mania 1' activity sheet for the full story

Other ideas

- Do 'Gecko Mania 1' craft on this page
- Have children draw their own geckos, mosquitos and other bugs
  - Display geckos climbing up the walls, over the ceiling or chasing each other around the room

Gecko mania!

Geckos are little lizards living in hot countries. Baby geckos are only 4cm long.

Geckos love to feast on delicious live insects such as flies, crickets and mosquitoes– yummy! At meal times they stick out their tongues to catch food as it flies past.

These very shy animals often hide in shady places under rocks.

Geckos love to live inside people's houses where they can find lots of places to hide. They can squeeze into cracks in the wall. Favourite hideouts are behind curtains and pictures.

Suction pads on their feet stop them falling off ceilings.

When *Geckos* live together they sometimes chase each other. If a *Gecko* is caught by its tail, the tail comes off giving him a chance to escape. Eventually another tail will grow — just like getting your second teeth.

What do you and the *Gecko* have in common? You are both small, shy, and stay at home!

What important job does the *Gecko* do? He eats mosquitoes that can carry malaria which is a nasty disease.

What important job can you do? Praying for missionaries is a *BIG* job you can do even if you're small.

Gecko shapes

Crafts

Chinese streamers

What is it?

Instructions for making streamers which can be used in a group activity.

What do you need?

- Smarties tubes or toilet rolls
- Crepe paper—at least three bright colours
- Scissors
- Sellotape
- Ruler
- Star stickers (silver/gold)
- String

What to do

Preparation

- Cut crepe paper into strips—about 1 metre long and 3cm wide. Cut three per child
- Cut smarties tube or toilet roll holder in half
- Cut one 30cm long length of string per child

On the day

- Give three streamers to every child
- Decorate streamers with stars
- Fold one end of each streamer into a point
- Tape the three points to the tube/toilet roll
- Thread string through tube and knot ends together
- Hold by string loop and wave in the air
- Experiment waving the streamer in a circle or make other shapes
- Wind the streamers round spool when not in use

What to say

In China children often wave streamers during parades. Today we are going to make our own Chinese streamers.

Other ideas

Appoint a leader. All copy how they wave their streamer. Change leaders.

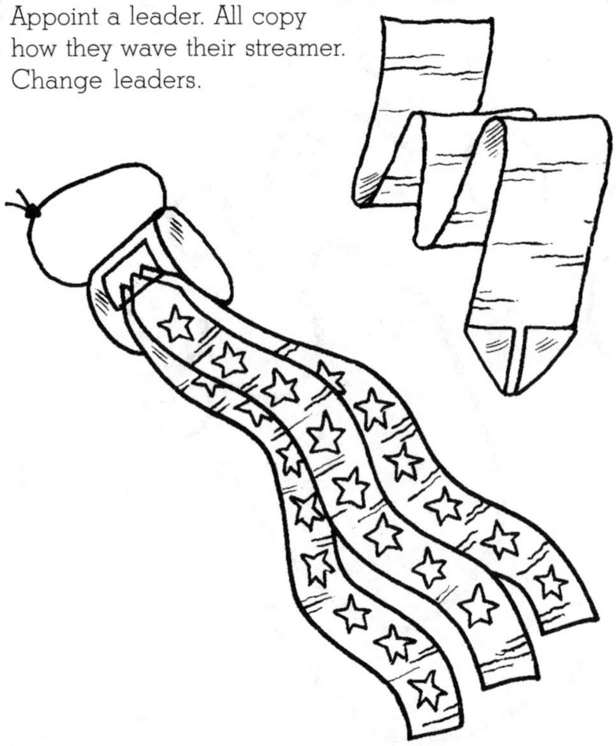

International face painting

What is it?

Guidelines for face painting using Asian flags as your theme.

It's a great way for children to learn the names of Asian countries and their flags. They are sure to take more than a passing interest in the one plastered all over their face!

What do you need?

These items can be bought from most craft and toy shops.

- Water-based make-up:
  - This is safe and easy to apply and remove
  - It comes off skin and clothes by simply using soap and water
  - Make sure you only use make-up paint specifically designed for the skin
- Sponges:
  - These are good for applying the base
  - After use wash in warm soapy water and rinse well
- Brushes. Use a variety of different sizes:
  - Small thin ones for detailed work
  - Medium sized ones for most areas
  - Large flat ones for big areas of colour
- Tissues for spills or mistakes
- Buckets or containers of clean water for rinsing brushes between colours
- Towels to cover the shoulders and clothes
- Headbands for tying hair back off the face

What to do?

- With a brush draw the outline of an Asian flag on the child's face. Consult encyclopedias, school books or the web
- Take care around the eyes. Ask the child to look up, away from the brush
- When painting over the eyelids ask the child not to screw up their face as it will make a mess and may get into their eyes
- Fill in the background colour with a sponge or a big brush
- Dip the sponge in water and give it a good squeeze before applying the make-up to it
- If it's too wet the make-up will streak unevenly
- If it's too dry the make-up will be difficult to apply

Other ideas

- Generate enthusiasm for this activity the previous week. Suggest they wear a bright top or t-shirt in a matching colour
- Bring your camera. This is a great individual or group photo opportunity. The final look will be totally stunning!
- Play team games based on countries

Pop-up jungle snake

What is it?

Instructions for making a pop-up snake card.

What do you need?

- Card—various colours
- Stiff paper—various colours including red
- Scissors
- Glue
- Felt tips or poster paint (and fine brushes)
+ Bead eyes (or use a hole punch and white paper)

What do you do?

Preparation

- Cut one 24cm x 12cm card per child
- Cut one 12cm diameter circle of card per child
- Cut one 11cm x 11cm squares of stiff paper per child (various colours)
- Make a sample card

On the day

- Fold cards in half—press hard to make a good crease
- Open folded card and stick one 11x11 square centrally on the right side
- Draw a snake's head in the centre of the circle of card. Draw the body in a continuous ring around this until you reach the edge
- Draw snake markings. Colour with felt tips or paint
- Cut along the line starting from the outside and working in
- Cut out a forked tongue (red paper). Glue it on the head
- Glue on beady eyes
- Glue half of the outer snake ring to the right side of the card
- Let the children write messages or draw on the front and back of the card to complete them
- When the card is opened, the snake will spring out!

What to say

Missionaries and missionary kids see different types of snakes in Asia. The colourful ones can be very poisonous! Invent your own snake and make it as dangerous as you like!

Other ideas

- Collect long, thin, twisty branches from the ground. Use poster paints to decorate these with snake-like markings. Display on a table.
- Cut out leaf shapes in green paper. Stick to the card before gluing in the snake, so that it appears to leap out from the jungle!

Japanese fan

What is it?

Instructions and patterns for making a Japanese fan.

What do you need?

- Thick card eg cereal boxes/cardboard
- Lollipop sticks
- Scissors
- Strong glue, stapler or sellotape
- Pencils, felt-tips and thick black marker
- White paper
- Photocopies of fan shape and patterns

What to do

Preparation

- Cut one 18cm square of card per child
- Photocopy fan shape on p 69. Glue on to card. Cut out. Use this template to make enough templates for one per four or five children.
- Photocopy the pictures below. Enlarge if desired. Make more than one per child so they can choose their favourite.
- Buy or collect lollipop sticks—one per child

On the day

- On the square card draw round the template
- Cut it out
- Colour in the photocopied pictures or design a simple Japanese drawing (eg a traditional character or Japanese handwriting)
- Cut out the pictures. (Younger children can cut along the dotted lines.) Stick them on to the fan. The broadest part of the fan is the top
- Glue, staple or sellotape lollipop stick to the base of the fan

What to say

When the weather is very hot Japanese people fan themselves with paper fans. The fans are called *uchiwa* (OO-chee-wah). They are made from split bamboo and Japanese paper called *washi* (WASH-ee). Designs are stencilled on.

Other ideas

- Serve ice lollies as treats. Wash the sticks. Allow to dry while children are making the fans. This also shows recycling can be fun!

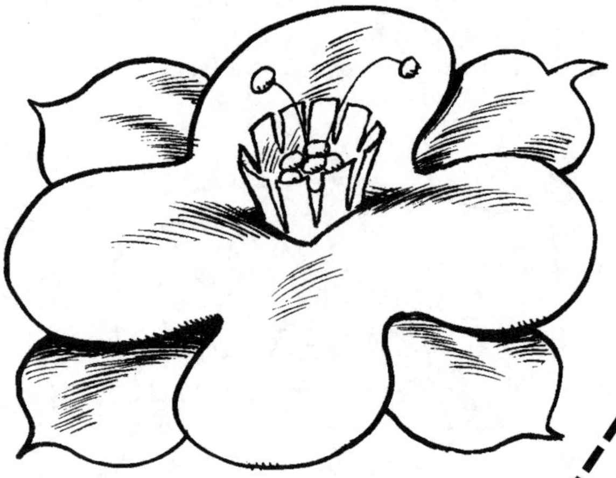

Japanese fan pattern

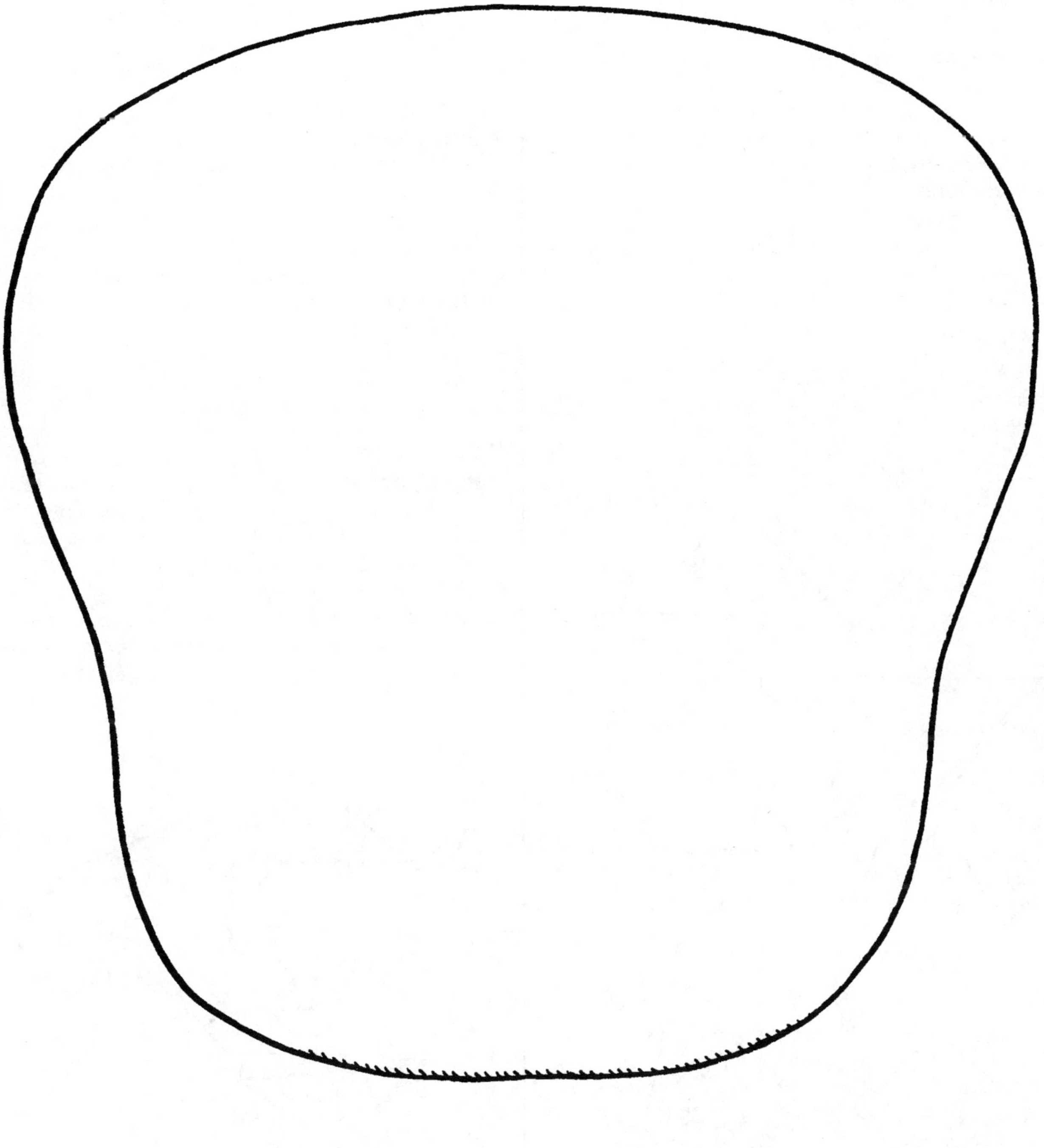

Note: The pictures on the facing page need to be enlarged if they are to be copied onto the fans.

Cats and dogs

What is it?

Instructions for simple origami.

What do you need?

- Coloured paper cut into squares
- Felt tip pens

What do you do?

Give each child two squares of paper

For the cat

- Fold the paper in half diagonally
- Fold the corners up for the ears closer to the centre than for the dog. Crease folds.
- Turn the paper over and draw a cat's face

For the dog

- Fold the paper in half diagonally
- Fold 2 narrow corner triangles, pointed ends down. Crease folds
- Draw the eyes and nose for a dog

Other ideas

Make the animal faces into pencil toppers. Simply stick them onto the top of the children's pencils using sellotape.

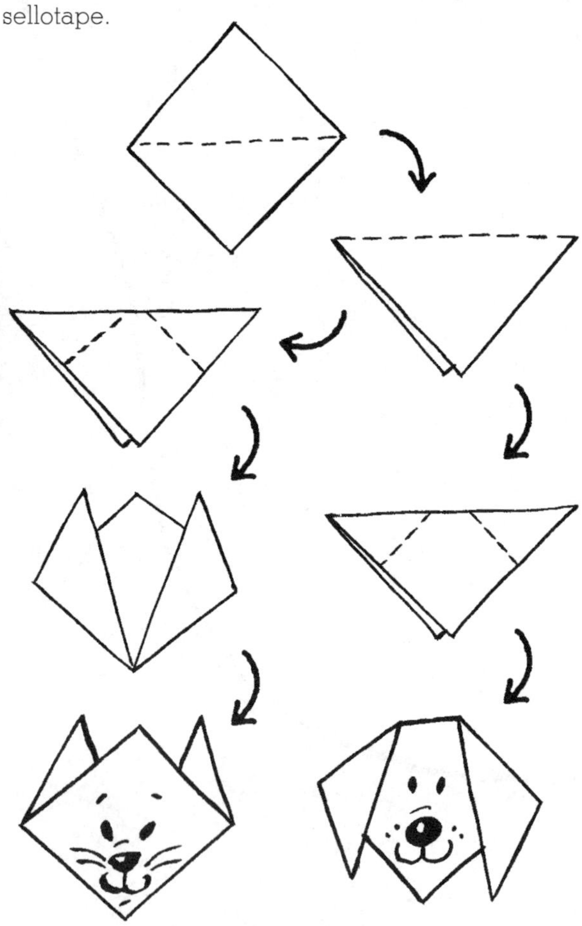

Jumping frogs!

What is it?

More complex instructions for making a jumping paper frog. Suitable for older children.

What do you need?

- A rectangle of paper
- Felt tip pens—red, blue, yellow, black
- Glue
- Paper for making eyes, or wobbly eyes

What do you do?

Preparation

- Buy or cut out suitable paper; at least one rectangle for each child
- Photocopy the instructions on p 71 so each child can see a copy
- Practice, so that you can make frogs yourself!

On the day

- Hand out materials
- Demonstrate
- Let the children make their own frogs
- Play a game with the finished frogs

Other ideas

Jumping game

- Cut out a large circle of blue paper for a pond. Cut smaller green circles. Cut a thin triangle out of each of these to make lily pads
- Try jumping frogs onto lily pads
- Score five points for landing on a lily pad near the edge of the pond, 10 for one near the centre, and take off five for landing in the wate. Give each child three goes and add up the scores.

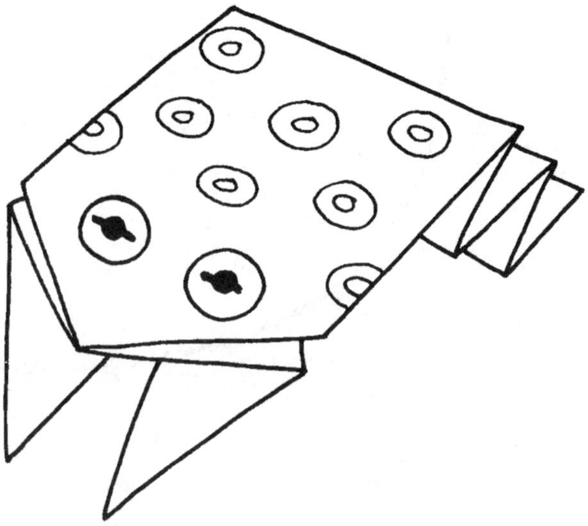

What is origami?

In Japan, many people like to fold paper to make different shapes and models. This kind of art is called origami [paper folding]. You can buy special paper for origami from art and craft stores. This is thin and easy to fold. You can also use newspaper, pages from old magazines, comics or wrapping paper.
For other ideas get an origami book from your local library or bookshop.

Jumping frogs!

1 Mark the top corners of the paper with a blue dot. Mark the bottom corners of the paper with a red dot. do this on both sides.

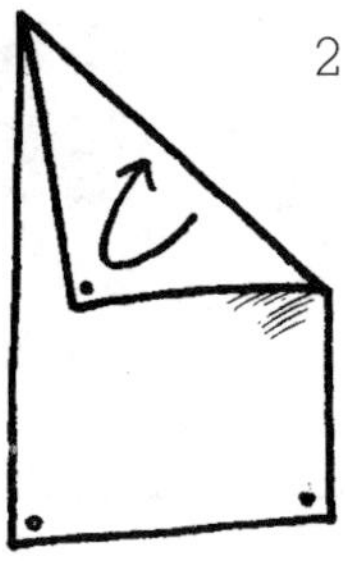

2 With the wrong side up, fold one blue corner across to the opposite edge then unfold it.

3 In the same way fold the other blue corner across to the opposite side. Then unfold it.

4 Mark the ends of the creases made in steps 2 and 3 with yellow dots. Do this on both sides of the paper.

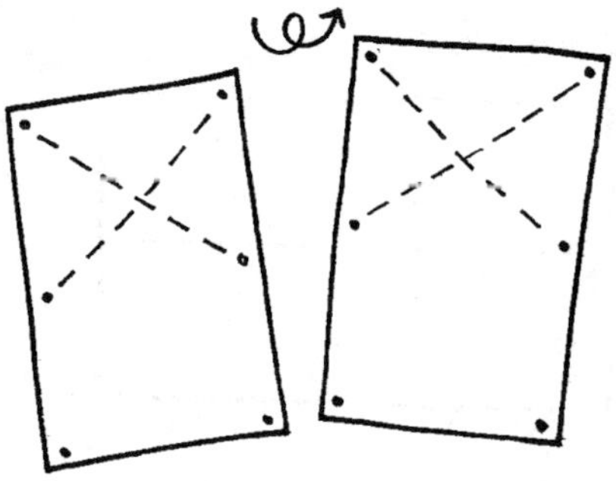

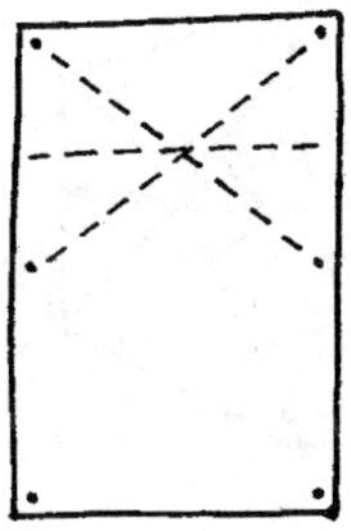

5 With the right side up, fold the edge with the blue corners down to the yellow dots. Then unfold it.

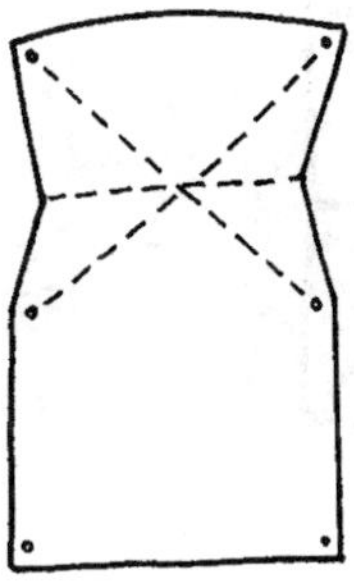

6 Put a finger at each end of the last crease and push gently inward (the middle should pop up).

7 Flatten the blue corners so they touch the yellow marks. Press this flap flat underneath.

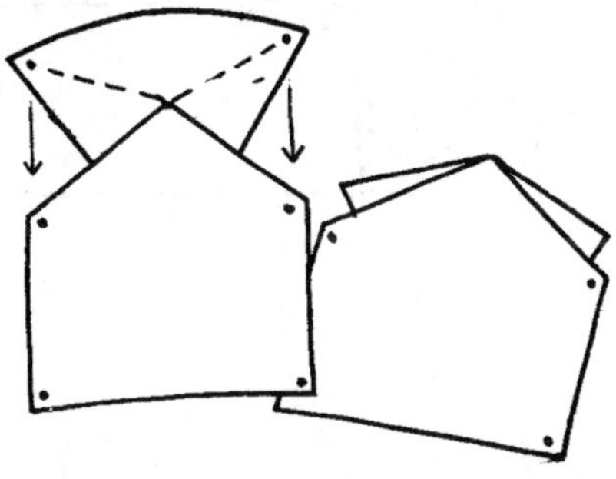

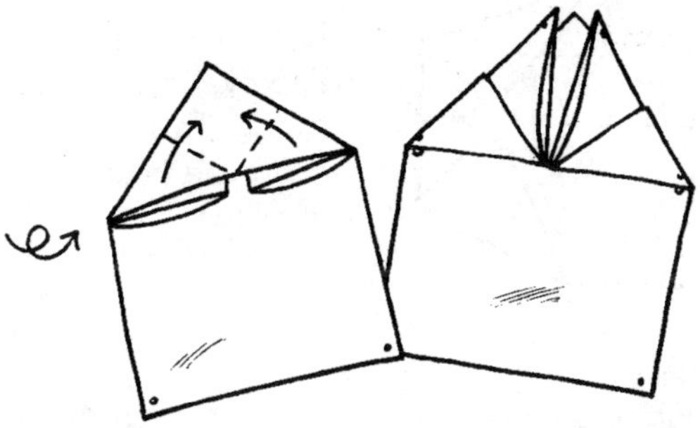

8 Turn the paper over. Fold the blue corners up to the point (this makes the front feet).

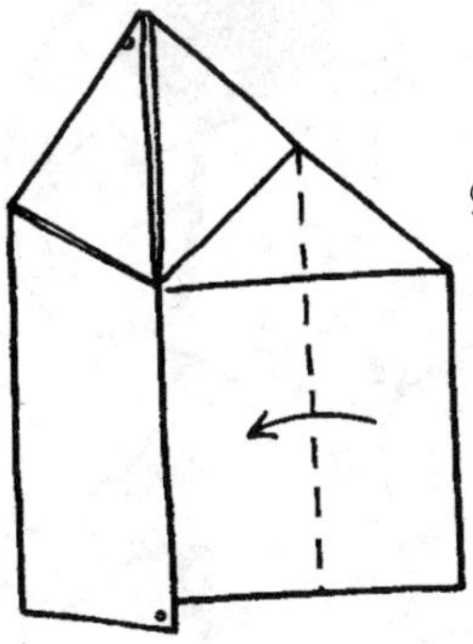

9 Fold in the right and left sides so they meet in the middle. Crease the folds well.

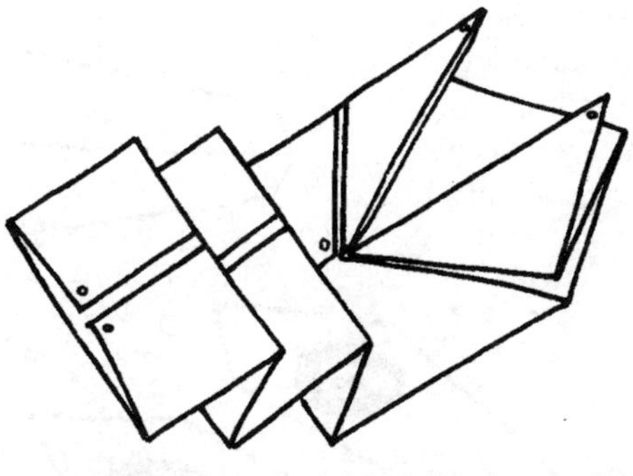

10 To make the back legs, fold at the base of the front feet. Fold back 1 cm, forward 1cm, and then back 1 cm. This creates a concertina style for the frog's back legs. Pull the front legs out a little so the frog can stand.

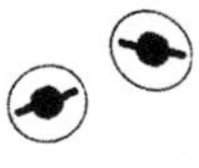

11 Draw black eyes on white circles and glue in place.

The Jet Set

What is it?

Instructions for making your own paper airplane. This one is an excellent glider.

What do you need?

- Coloured A4 paper
- Photocopies of this page, eg one between two

What do you do?

Follow the instructions!

Other ideas

- Add designs to your plane, eg name of airline, symbol or flag
- Play 'Fasten your seatbelts' (p 80)

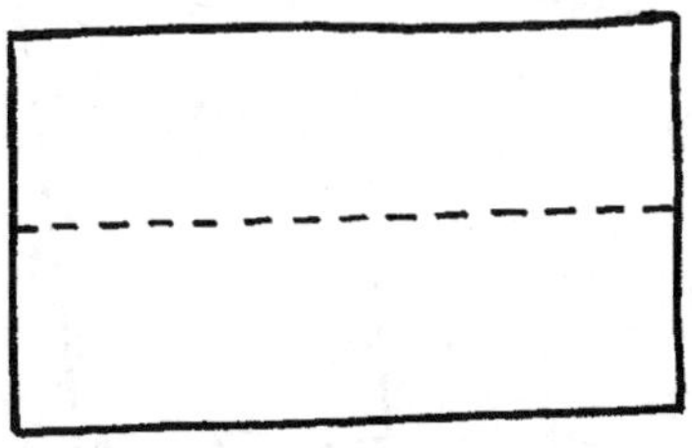

1 Fold paper along the middle. Unfold again.

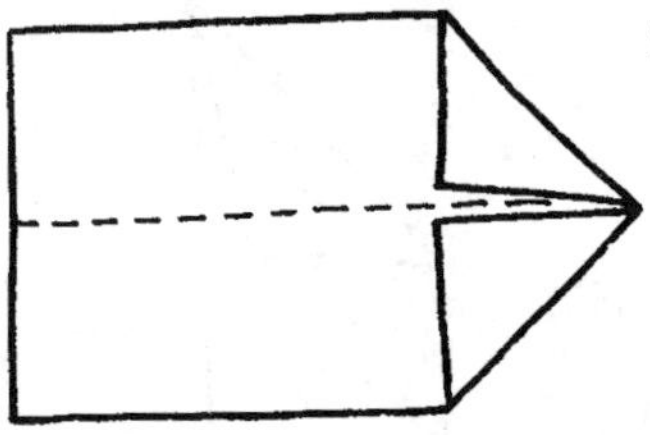

2 Fold the bottom corners in to meet the middle crease.

3 Turn your paper over. Fold the point of the triangle into the middle.

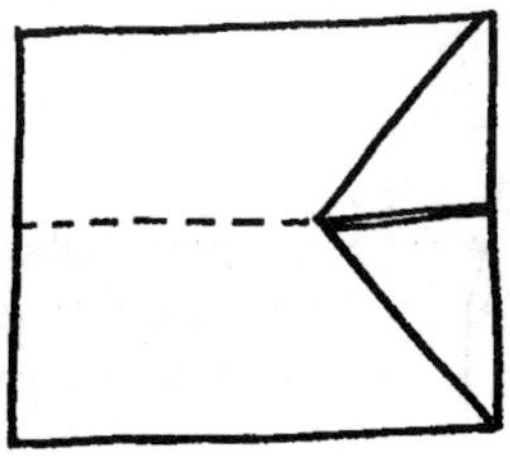

4 Fold the corners of the paper into the middle line so a little flap is still visible.

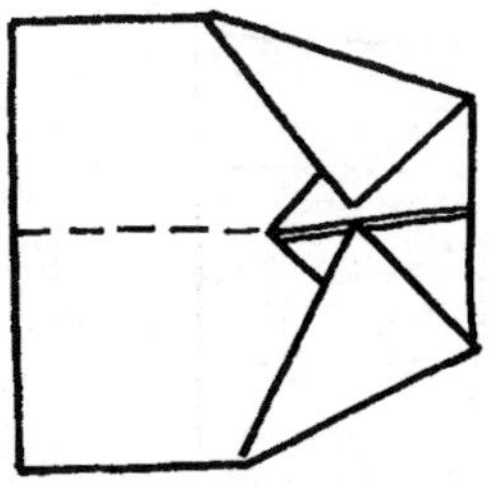

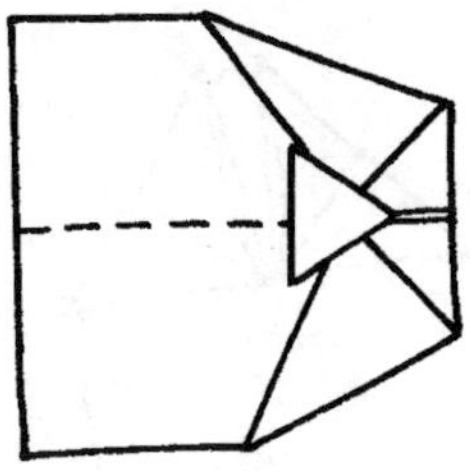

5 Fold this small flap over the wings. This holds the folds in place.

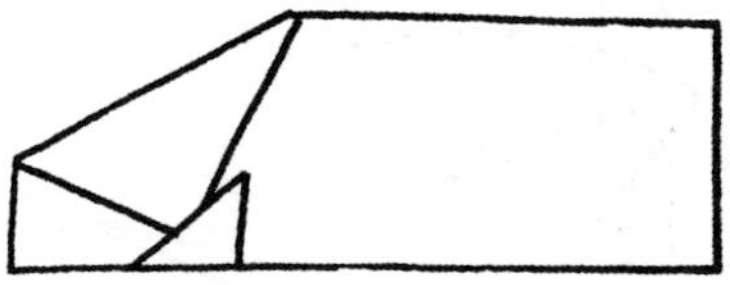

6 Turn the paper over and fold back along the middle line. You should see the little triangle at the bottom.

7 Fold the edge of the wing down so that it lies on the bottom edge of the paper. Do the same for the other wing, then unfold the wings slightly.

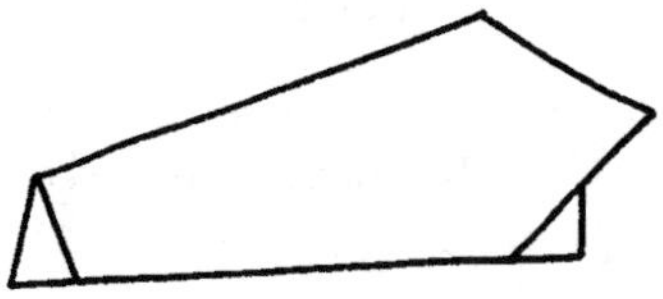

[top view]

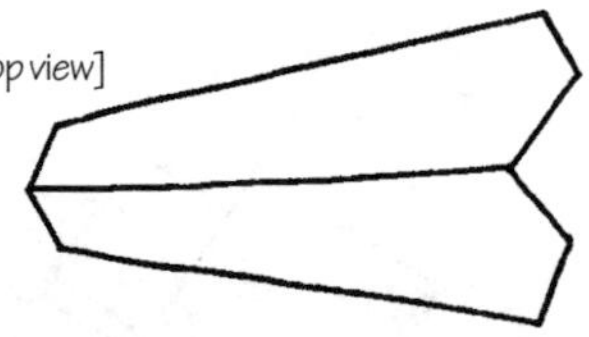

8 Now you're ready to fly! Hold the triangle and gently push the glider into the air!

Write on!

What is it?

A worksheet for practicing Chinese script.

What do you need?

- Photocopies of the worksheet (p 74)
- Pens, pencils for the script
- \+ Coloured pens, crayons for colouring in

What do you do?

Preparation

- Photocopy one worksheet per child

On the day

- Give out copies of the worksheet
- Demonstrate how to write the characters
- Let the children complete the worksheets at their own pace

This is also a good activity to have up your sleeve for early finishers.

What to say

- All Chinese learn to write by drawing these characters. There are thousands to remember!
- Christian workers in China, wanting to communicate with Chinese people, have to learn to draw the characters! That's very hard work!

Other ideas

- See if anyone can remember off by heart how to draw some of the difficult characters! Have a competition to see who does best!
- On paper, draw characters from memory. See whose is best and give a prize.
- On a blackboard, have pairs of volunteers draw a character from memory. See who can finish first and whose looks best.
- 'Wang Li Bing' (p 46)
- 'How to pray for new missionaries' (p 55)

Japanese wordsearch

What is it?

A wordsearch handout on Japan.

What do you need?

- Photocopies of wordsearch handout (p 75)
- Pens/pencils
- \+ Coloured pens, crayons for colouring in

What do you do?

- Hand out photocopies and pens
- Let the children find the names!
- Early finishers can colour in the pictures!

This is also a very useful 'filler' item. Have copies ready for those who complete other activities early.

Other ideas

- 'Where on earth...?' (p 60)
- Hashimoto (p 44)

Solution

N	H	A	K	O	D	A	T	E	O	F	R
A	O	Y	O	S	H	I	K	O	K	U	N
G	N	P	B	A	O	M	O	R	I	J	A
O	S	S	E	N	D	A	I	M	H	I	G
Y	H	O	K	K	A	I	D	O	W	J	A
A	U	K	Y	U	S	H	U	S	L	A	S
K	A	G	O	S	H	I	M	A	T	P	A
K	A	M	A	K	U	R	A	K	O	A	K
S	M	I	Y	A	J	I	M	A	K	N	I
Y	O	K	O	H	A	M	A	X	Y	C	V
K	Y	O	T	O	S	A	P	P	O	R	O

Crafts

Write on... in Chinese!

You need to be able to draw Chinese characters in the right order. Can you draw them?

one (yi)	一		two (er)	一	二		ten (shi)	一	十	

Chinese characters have been around for thousands of years. Probably they started as drawings, and were simplified into the characters used today. Some still look like the first drawings might have looked. Some characters are easy. Try drawing these.

man (ren)			丿	人						
fire (huo)	丿	人	火 (partial)	火						
tree (mu)	一	十	才	木						
mountain (shan)		丨	山 (partial)	山						

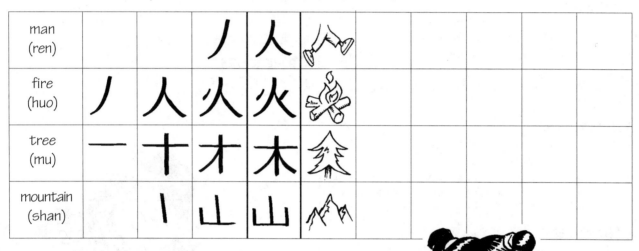

In Chinese, there are more than 50,000 characters! At school, you only have to learn 26 letters to make up our alphabet. If you were in China, you'd have to memorise how to draw more than 5,000 before you left primary school!

Some characters are quite difficult. Try drawing these.

God (shen)		丶	ラ	ネ	ネ	礻	礻冂	礻冃	礻日	神
神										
is (shi)		丨	冂	冃	日	旦	早	早	昰	是
是										
love (ai)	一	⺈	⺈丶	⺈丶丶	爫	爫 (partial)	爫冖	爱 (partial)	爱 (partial)	爱
爱										

Japanese wordsearch

N	H	A	K	O	D	A	T	E	O	F	R
A	O	Y	O	S	H	I	K	O	K	U	N
G	N	P	B	A	O	M	O	R	I	J	A
O	S	S	E	N	D	A	I	M	H	I	G
Y	H	O	K	K	A	I	D	O	W	J	A
A	U	K	Y	U	S	H	U	S	L	A	S
K	A	G	O	S	H	I	M	A	T	P	A
K	A	M	A	K	U	R	A	K	O	A	K
S	M	I	Y	A	J	I	M	A	K	N	I
Y	O	K	O	H	A	M	A	X	Y	C	V
K	Y	O	T	O	S	A	P	P	O	R	O

Other cities

1 Sapporo
2 Hakodate
3 Aomori
4 Sendai
5 Kamakura
6 Yokohama
7 Fuji (mountain)
8 Nagoya
9 Kyoto
10 Osaka
11 Kobe
12 Miyajima
13 Nagasaki
14 Kagoshima

There are 20 Japanese names in this wordsearch. Underline them as you find them.

Sing in another language

What is it?
Asian words for familiar choruses.

What do you need?
- Overhead projector, blackboard or large piece of paper to write the songs on
- Guitar/piano to accompany

What to do
Preparation
- Pick the song that fits the theme of your session
- Practice so you feel happy to teach it. Teach your helpers first so that you sing as a choir
- Write it out on an OHP slide, blackboard or large piece of paper so that the children can read it

On the day
- Introduce the song. Sing the English version first
- Read the Asian version a line at a time. Have the children repeat each line. It doesn't matter if your pronunciation isn't perfect!
- Sing the Asian version
- Point to the words as you sing. Then they and you shouldn't get lost!

What to say
People all over the world like to sing. As Christians, we want to praise God with our songs.

Sometimes when English songs are translated into other languages, the words don't quite fit the music. They can be difficult to sing.

We need to pray for
- Skilled translators who can get the meaning of English songs into the local language. (They can translate English songs, but it is best if they write songs in their own language and with the music of their country. The singing is not then 'foreign'.)
- Local Christians to write praise songs in their own language

Other ideas
- Pray for Asian Christians (p 57)

Chinese: God is so good

Shen jiu shi ai	*God is love*
Shen jiu shi ai	*God is love*
Shen jiu shi ai	*God is love*
Ta zhe yang ai wo	*This is how he loves me*
Chui ting wo qiu	*He answers prayer*
Chui ting wo qiu	*He answers prayer*
Chui ting wo qiu	*He answers prayer*
Ta zhe yang ai wo	*This is how he loves me*
Ta shi wo zhu	*He is my Lord*
Ta shi wo zhu	*He is my Lord*
Ta shi wo zhu	*He is my Lord*
Ta zhe yang ai wo	*This is how he loves me*
Ta kuai zai lai	*He's coming again soon*
Ta kuai zai lai	*He's coming again soon*
Ta kuai zai lai	*He's coming again soon*
Ta zhe yang ai wo	*This is how he loves me*

Japanese: God is so good
Shu wa subarashii
Shu wa subarashii
Shu wa subarashii
Watashi no Shu

Indonesian: This is the day
Hari ini, hari ini
Harinya Tuhan, harinya Tuhan
Mari kita, mari kita
Bersukaria, bersukaria
Hari ini harinya Tuhan
Mari kita bersukaria
Hari ini
Hari ini harinya Tuhan

Thai: This is the day
Wanee ben wan, wanee ben wan
Tee Prajaw song sang, tee Prajaw song sang,
Hai rao yindee, hai rao yindee
Leoo boek ban nai jai, leoo boek ban nai jai
Wanee ben wan tee prajaw song sang
Hai rao yindee leoo boek ban nai jai
Wanee ben wan, wanee ben wan
Tee Prajaw song sang

Tagalog: This is the day
(the Philippines)
Ito ang araw, ito ang araw
Na gawa ng Diyos, na gawa ng Diyos
Tayo magsaya, tayo magsaya
At purihin siya, at purihin siya
Ito ang araw na gawa ng Diyos
Tayo magsaya at purihin siya
Ito ang araw
Ito ang araw na gawa ng Diyos

Games

Contents

Wakey, wakey!

What is it?
A game for settling children down.

What do you need?
Nothing!

What do you do
- Choose someone to be 'it'
- Other children lie down on the floor and pretend to be asleep
- Make sure they're all snoring loudly and no peeping!
- The player who is 'it' quietly tiptoes and taps a sleeping child on the shoulder
- The one tapped gets up without making a noise, joins hands with the first child
- The one who is 'it' taps another child who joins the chain of wide awake children
- The chain gets longer and longer with the player who was 'it' still at the front
- Keep going (on tiptoe, remember!) until only one player is left sleeping
- The chain forms a circle around the sleepy head
- At the top of their voices they shout 'Wakey, wakey!'
- This child can now be 'it' and you can play again!

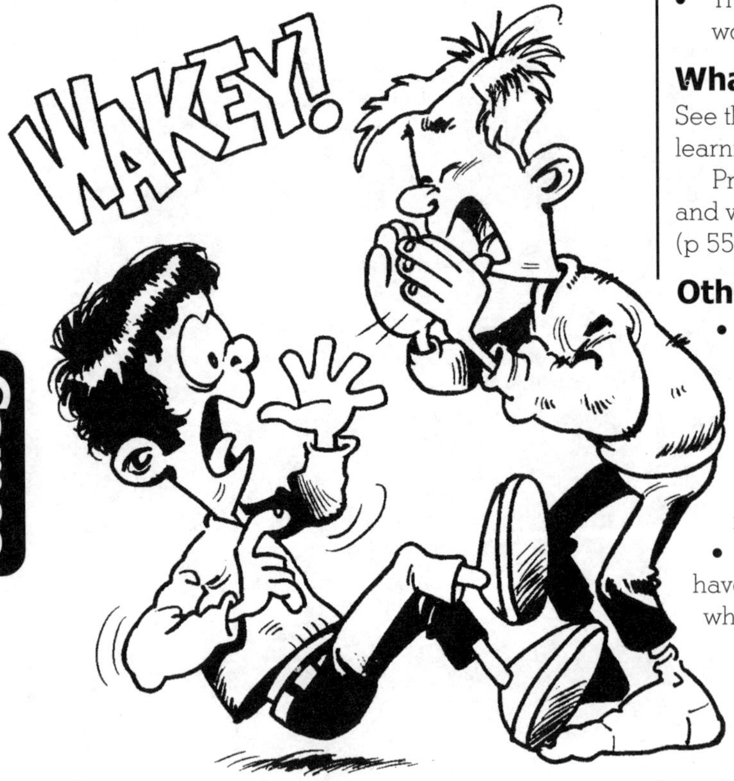

What to say
If you live in a hot Asian country early morning is the best part of the day because it's cool (well... cool-*er*!) Children usually get up about 5.30am and have eaten their breakfast by 6.00! Sometimes they like to exercise or play sport. Perhaps they need to help their family in the fields before they go to school and the sun gets too hot. Some just like to get a bit of extra swotting in! See Hashimoto (p 44).

I packed my bag...

What is it?
A memory game. What do you need to take with you if you go to Asia as a missionary? Or what would you miss?

What do you need?
- Nothing

What do you do?
- Sit the children in a circle
- Pretend you are going to fly to Asia as a missionary. (If possible pick a country of a missionary they know.)
- Think up something you need to take
- The first child starts: 'I packed my bag for [Asia] and I took...'
- Other children list the items already mentioned by previous children, plus one more they would take

Example
- First child: 'I packed my bag for China and I took my bicycle'
- Second child: 'I packed my bag for China and I took my bicycle and my lego set'
- Third child: 'I packed my bag for China and I took my bicycle, my lego set and my Bible'
- The sentence gets longer until someone forgets a word!

What to say:
See the action sheets on culture shock and language learning (p 18-20).

Pray for new missionaries as they settle in to new and very different countries. See 'How to pray...' (p 55).

Other ideas
- Older children could choose things they think they'd miss; things they might not be able to get in [Asia]. Eg 'I went to [Thailand] and I wish I had [some chocolate].' It doesn't matter whether or not you can get chocolate in Thailand—the game is just to heighten awareness of living in a different country
- Younger children need not repeat what others have packed. They simply have to 'pack' something which has not yet been mentioned

Shoe scramble

What is it?
An ice breaker.

What do you need?
- A blindfold for each player

What do you do
- Divide children into small teams of 4-10
- Each team sits in a circle
- Players take their shoes off and throw them into the middle of the circle
- Blindfold each player and mix up the shoes
- On the word '**SCRAMBLE**' players dive into the middle and try and find their own shoes
- The winners are the team to finish first with all the right shoes on!

What to say
In many parts of Asia, people take their shoes off before they come into a house. A big pile of shoes outside your front door tells your neighbours you have a lot of visitors! The fun starts when they all decide to leave at the same time and its a mad scramble to work out whose shoes are whose.

Toilet game

What is it?
A quick game for an unlimited number of children.

What do you need?
- Paper
- Blu-tack

What do you do?
Preparation

- Write the names for toilets on separate sheets of paper (see below and p 94)
- You may want to use the symbols for boys/girls on additional sheets behind the Asian words so as to be able to reveal the 'answers' (templates on p 94)

On the day
- Stick up the pairs of words with blu-tack, just above head height (or write them on a blackboard)
- Explain these are the names for boys and girls toilets in a different language. As a new missionary, you have to know which is which!
- Give children 10 seconds to line up behind the sign they think is right for them
- 'Are you sure?' Give them one last chance to change their minds
- Reveal which is for boys and which is for girls. Who would be embarassed!?
- Let them sit down, and repeat

Country	Girls	Boys
Thailand	Ying	Chay
Indonesia	Wanita	Pria
Vietnam	Nữ	Nam
Malaysia	Perempuan	Laki-laki
Philippines	Babae	Lalaki

see p 94 for Chinese characters

What to say
New missionaries have a hard time because everything is new—even the day to day simple things. Not being able to speak the language or know what to do in a new country is just like being a baby all over again.
- Pray for a missionary you know (see p 55)

Fasten your seatbelts!

What is it?

A game using paper airplanes.

What do you need?

- Paper aeroplanes (see craft at p 72)
- Colouring pens
- Flags (from an encyclopaedia or the web)
- Hula hoops or string

What do you do?

- Children write their name on their airplane
- Divide into four teams. Send the teams to different corners of the room
- Give each team the name of an Asian country. All team members draw the flag of that country on their plane. (If time is limited, or for younger children, use a colour coding system or stickers.)
- Place five or six hula hoops or circles of string in the middle of the floor. Name each one after a capital city in Asia eg:
    - Seoul (Korea), Taipei (Taiwan), Beijing (China), Jakarta (Indonesia), Manila (Philippines)
- These hoops are airports
- Say: 'Ladies and gentlemen, please fasten your seatbelts.' Children get ready to throw their planes
- Say: 'You are now landing at Taipei International airport.' Children try to get their planes into the right hoop. They must not leave their corner, and only one throw is allowed
- Award points according to the number of planes in the hoop
- Say: 'Thank you for flying with [your church's name] Airlines.' Children run and find their own plane and return to their corner
- Play again

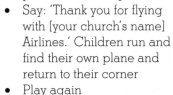

What to say

For many missionaries, travelling long distances is a way of life. Some flights take all day or night but the passengers are treated well with meals and movies to watch. They see many different places around the world and often have lots of adventures to tell!

Dressing-up

What is it?

A game of luck and skill using dice and chopsticks! Suitable for 5-60 players.

What do you need?

- two dice
- a bag of Maltesers
- plastic bowl
- chopsticks
- bathrobe/dressing gown
- scarf
- hat
- kids sunglasses
- slippers

What do you do?

On the day

- Put Maltesers into the bowl with chopsticks and clothes beside it.
- Position the children in a circle around the bowl (two metres away)

How to play

- Take it in turns to throw the dice
- When a double six is thrown, run to the pile of clothes, put them on (on top of their own) as quickly as possible. Pick up the chopsticks and begin eating the Maltesers—no hands allowed!
- As soon as another double six is thrown, player one must stop, take off the dressing-up clothes and return to his place in the circle
- Player two gets into the clothes and eats Maltesers with chopsticks
- The game ends when the bowl is empty!

At the market stall

What is it?

Directions for a role play—trying to haggle/bargain with play money (Chinese yuan).

What do you need?

- photocopies of Chinese money
- plastic or real items for your stall—fruit, vegetables, chocolate, treats the children can eat, etc...

Preparation

- Copy, cut out and colour in the paper money. Use different colours for the different value notes. You may wish to involve helpers from your class!

On the day

- Set up the stall on a table
- Ask for two volunteers. One is the buyer and the other is the seller.
- Give both the children some Chinese yuan to use in the exchange
- Bargain away!

What to say

- Explain to the seller that the item will not keep and must be sold today. The seller needs to encourage the buyer by praising the item and the bargain price being asked. Tell the seller to start at 20 yuan if he wants to sell the item at 15.
- Explain to the buyer that the item is always priced too high at first and he must make up several reasons why it should be reduced in price. The buyer should start at half the price asked (10 yuan) and gradually offer more yuan as the seller brings down his price.
- The more dramatic the argument, the more fun it is to watch, but remember it is only a game and the fight is a pretend one!

Mango, Mango, Durian!

What is it?
A game to warm them up or puff them out!

What do you need?
Nothing

What do you do?
- Choose one child to be 'it'
- Other children form a big circle and sit down on the floor
- The child who is 'it' walks around the outside of the circle tapping each child (gently!) on the head and saying 'mango'
- As soon as the child taps someone's head and says 'durian' the child on the floor jumps up and chases 'it' around the circle until they get back to the space where they started
- If the second child catches 'it' before he or she sits down then 'it' has to go again
- If the second child can't catch 'it' he starts the game again
- Play as many times as you like or until lots of children have had a go

What to say?
The mango and the durian are both very popular and delicious fruits in Asia. Unfortunately, there is one problem with the durian. It smells like a stink bomb on the outside but tastes like sweet custard on the inside! Some people say the smell reminds them of a bin lorry squashing a lump of rotten cheese on a very damp day! Yuk. So if you sniff a cartload of durians at the market you might want to run a mile! In most countries it is illegal to carry durian on planes or on the underground.

Sadly (or not so sadly!) supermarkets here don't stock durians but they should have mangoes in their tropical fruit section.

Other Ideas
You could play a similar game using 'Gecko, gecko, crocodile!' instead. Read all about cute little geckos (p 64).

Chop Suey!

What is it?
Another game to warm children up/puff them out while helping them to learn the names of different Asian countries.

What do you need?
- Enough chairs for every child except one.
- A list of names of East Asian countries

What do you do?
- Choose one child to be 'it'
- Other children bring their chairs into a big circle
- Take the names of four Asian countries and go around the children giving each of them a country For example: 'Thailand, Mongolia, Vietnam, Singapore, Thailand, Mongolia, Vietnam, Singapore....' Also give 'it' a country
- Tell them to remember their country (each child keeps the same name for the whole game)
- The child who is 'it' stands in the middle of the circle and calls out one of the countries, eg 'Singapore!'
- All the children with that name jump off their chairs, run and sit down on another one (they are not allowed to go back to their own chair)
- The child in the middle also runs and tries to sit on an empty chair
- The one left without a chair is then 'it' and you play again (and again!)
- If the child in the middle shouts 'Chop Suey!' things get a little bit crazier. Everyone has to jump up and change to another chair!

What to say?
Chop Suey is a yummy noodle dish made with anything you fancy and all stir-fried together. It is eaten by Chinese people all over Asia... and the world. Check it out at your local Chinese take-away!

Other Ideas
If you have time, combine this with the Face Painting (p 66). You'd have to limit yourself to four different flags but you'd certainly end up with a very colourful game!

Presohan

What is it?
A game of catch from the Philippines.

What do you need?
- Masking tape
- Measuring tape
- Felt pens
- Empty Coca-Cola/Fanta cans

What do you do?
Preparation
- Use masking tape (or chalk) to mark a small X on the ground
- Put a small piece of masking tape on each can
- Mark a line about 2.5 metres from the X

On the day
- Give each player an empty can
- Children write their name on the masking tape on their can
- Choose one player to be the prisoner
- The prisoner sets his or her can on the X and stands behind it
- Players stand behind the line and take turns throwing their can at the prisoner's can
- Once a player hits the prisoner's can, the hitter must try to retrieve his can without being caught by the prisoner
- The prisoner cannot catch the hitter until he has put his own can back on the X
- Once the hitter crosses the line he is safe in the den
- If the hitter is caught he or she becomes the prisoner
- If a player throws but does not hit the prisoner's can he or she must wait
- when someone hits the can, all players who have missed try to grab their can and run back across the line without being caught by the prisoner

Other Ideas
Before or after playing this game, learn about Donnalyn, a little girl from the Philippines (p 48).

Lame chicken

What is it?
A Chinese relay game

What do you need?
- 20 sticks about 60 cm long
- chalk or tape

What do you do?
Preparation
- Place 10 sticks on the ground parallel to each other and about 30 cm apart
- Use chalk or tape to mark a starting line about five metres from the first stick
- Make an identical course with the other 10 sticks

On the day
- Divide the children into two even teams
- Teams stand in single file behind starting line
- Decide whether children should hop on one foot or two (depending on age of group)
- Shout 'go!' The first player on each team hops up to the first stick and over each stick, picking up the last one
- Player then hops back over each stick holding the stick that was picked up. This is then placed about 30 cm in front of the first stick
- Player then hops back to tag the next player in line
- The next player then goes
- The first team to have all their players complete the course wins

Other Ideas
Use this game while learning about a Chinese boy called Wang Li Bing (p 46).

The Great Crab Race

What is it?
A Japanese relay race.

What do you need?
Nothing

What do you do?
- Line children up in four equal teams at one end of the room
- On 'Go!' the first player gets down on hands and knees and crawls sideways to the far end of the room and back
- The next crawls backwards for their run
- The third crawls sideways, the fourth backwards, and so on to the end of the line
- The first team to have all their players back and standing in a straight line are the winners.

What to say?
Have you ever watched a crab scurry across the beach? It will go sideways and backwards but rarely forwards. The Japanese prefer to see crabs not on the beach but on the menu! Crab meat is a favourite dish in Japan.

The Great Peanut Race

What is it?
A relay race using chopsticks and peanuts.

What do you need?
- Four pairs of chopsticks
- Big bag of peanuts
- Eight saucers

What do you do?
- Divide children into four even teams
- Place an empty saucer opposite each team at the other end of the room
- Fill the other saucers with one peanut per team member. Set these saucers at the starting line in front of each team
- The first person on each team holds the chopsticks. On the word 'Go!' pick up a peanut and carry it to the saucer at the other end of the room
- Dash back and hand the chopsticks to the next person
- Players are not allowed to use their hands. If they drop a peanut they have to pick it up with their chopsticks
- First team to have all their players finish and in a straight line are the winners

What to say?
To find out more about chopsticks and how to use them (p 86).

The drinking game

What is it?
A relay race with cups of drinking water. A good game to finish on if children are thirsty after running around. They may need a toilet break after this one!

What do you need?
- A plastic cup for each child
- Drinking water
- Four towels

What do you do?
- Divide the children into four even teams.
- Stand in lines and give each a plastic cup of water (equal amounts of water in each)
- Drape a towel over the shoulders of the first person on each team
- On 'Go!' the first person drinks all the water from their cup as quickly as possible, turns it upside down on their head and passes the towel to the next in line
- When the first cup is empty and in position the second player can start drinking
- The first team to have everyone with a beaker on their head wins

What to say?
If you were going to live in a hot Asian country the doctor would probably advise you to drink three litres of water a day to stay healthy. That's about 24 plastic cups of water per person every day!

Jan-Ken-Pon

What is it?
In English, scissors-paper-stone. This was originally a Japanese game. Use this to see who has to do the clearing up!

What do you need?
Nothing.

What do you do?
Practise making the following shapes with your hands:
- **Scissors:** Forefinger and middle finger straight and spread apart, with the other fingers and thumb bent
- **Paper:** Hand opened flat
- **Stone:** Make a fist

The players divide into pairs or groups of three or four:
- Players put one hand behind their backs
- Together chant, 'Jan-Ken-Pon'
- At the same time, bring hands from behind backs and show what you have chosen (no cheating!)

Who wins?
- Paper beats stone because it can cover a stone
- Stone beats scissors because it can break scissors
- Scissors beat paper because they can cut paper

This can be played as a knockout, or as the first to win 10 games.

Other ideas
- Where on earth...? (p 60)
- Kids like me — Hashimoto (p 44)

How to use chopsticks

What is it?

Instructions for using chopsticks.

What do you do?

Part 1

- Use whatever hand you write with
- Slot the thick end of one chopstick in the hollow between your thumb and first finger
- Rest the middle of the chopstick firmly on your third finger
- This is the base chopstick and does not move

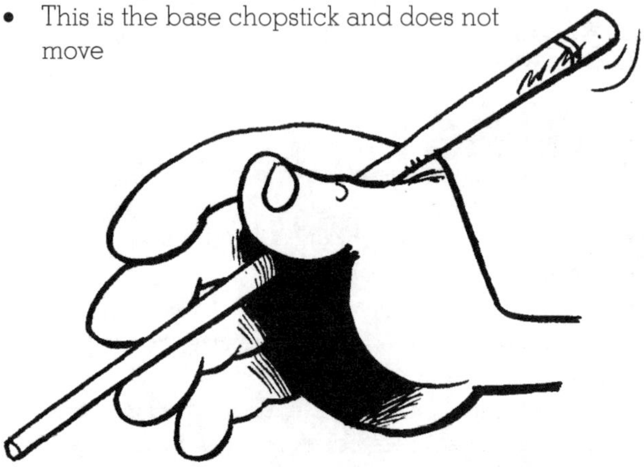

Part 2

- Hold the second chopstick between your thumb and first and second fingers, similar to the way you hold a pencil
- Move your first finger and thumb to wiggle the top chopstick up and down. (It should look like a snapping crocodile!)
- Make sure the tips of your chopsticks are even. Now see if you can pick up something bite-sized and get it into your mouth
- Start off with popcorn or pasta. Try Maltesers, peanuts or Smarties (the hardest of all!)

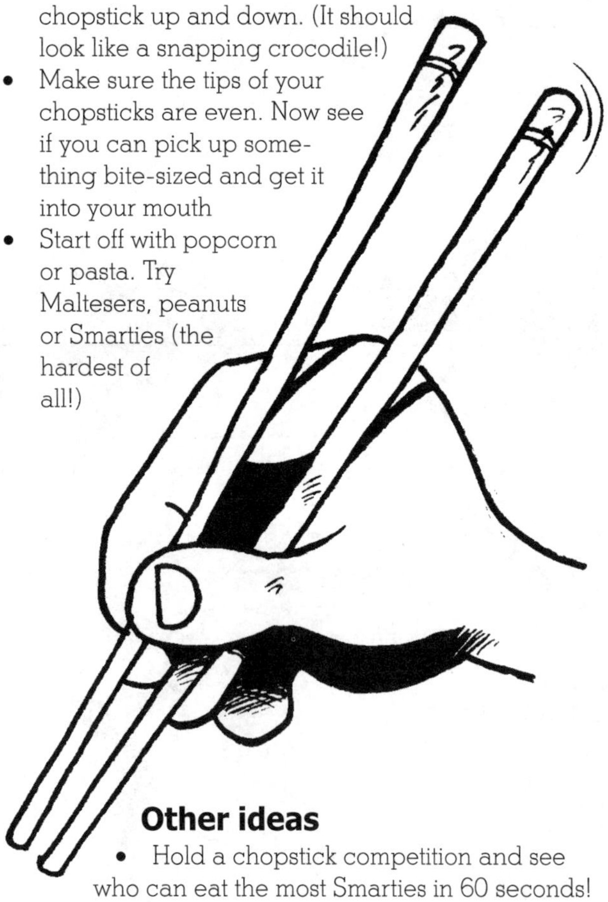

Other ideas

- Hold a chopstick competition and see who can eat the most Smarties in 60 seconds!
- Try playing the 'Dressing-up game' (p 80).

Munch, munch, you're lunch!

What is it?

A big challenge party game. Players have to cross a raging river on a plank without being eaten by crocodiles.

What do you need?

- A plank
- Five or six inflated balloons
- A blindfold

What do you do?

- Lay the plank on the floor and place the inflated balloons at the far end
- Tell the children to pretend there is a raging river below the plank and a big canyon where the balloons are
- Each player must cross the plank blindfolded and jump the canyon at the end (if they fall off the plank or burst a balloon they are out)
- Blindfold the first volunteer. Other children can pretend to be hungry crocodiles swimming around in the river
- They all shout 'Munch, munch, you're lunch' as the player tries to get from one end to the other but they are not allowed to touch him
- Take turns
- Whoever crosses the raging river without getting eaten by crocodiles or falling in the canyon at the end is a winner!

What to say?

Missionaries in remote areas often have to cope with bad roads and hazardous travelling. Sometimes they have to cross swinging bridges or slippery logs laid across a stream. How good do you think you would be at that?

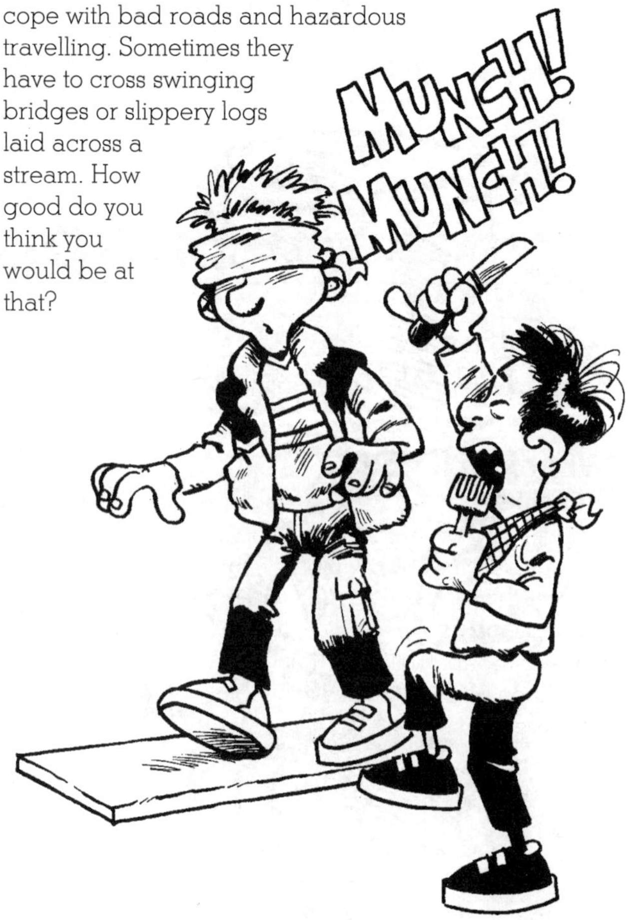

Snacks and recipes

Contents

Shopping list

What is it?

A list of some traditional Asian snacks to look out for at your local supermarket.

What you'll find

Munchies

- Phileas Fogg Indonesian Crackers: Lemon Grass and Coriander or Sambal flavour
- Boulevard Japanese Rice Crackers

Packet soups

- Knorr Soups of the World, Thai Chicken and Lemon Grass or Malaysian Chicken and Sweetcorn

Packet noodles

- Crosse and Blackwell 3-minute noodles, Oriental Beef or Chinese Chicken

Frozen Stir Fries

- Oriental Express Stir Fry, Egg Fried Rice or Chinese Noodles

Teas

- Check out the Tea/Coffee aisle for selections of Japanese and Chinese tea

Other ideas

Keep exploring those shelves and you'll find so much more!

Chinese fried rice

What is it?
A recipe for fried rice. This makes 5-6 small helpings. Just double up (or treble up!) depending on numbers and how hungry everyone is!

What do you need?
- 375g/12 oz cooked rice
- 6 mushrooms
- 150g/5oz bean sprouts
- 6 iceberg lettuce leaves or Chinese leaves if you can get them
- 120g/4oz frozen peas
- 6 spring onions
- 1 garlic clove, peeled and crushed
- 1 tsp grated fresh ginger or 1 tbs, if dried
- 3 tbs soy sauce
- 3 tbs vegetable oil (groundnut oil is best)

\+ Optional: prawns, pieces of cooked chicken, tuna

What do you do?
- Slice mushrooms
  Cut lettuce leaves into thin strips
  With your knife at a slant, slice the spring onions into 2 cm slices
- Heat the oil in a wok or frying pan
  Add garlic and ginger and fry for 30 seconds
  Stir all the time
- Add mushrooms and fry for 2 minutes
  Stir in spring onions, peas, lettuce, rice and bean sprouts

\+ Optional: add prawns, pieces of cooked chicken or tuna
  Keep everything moving on a high heat
- Sprinkle soy sauce in and stir-fry for 5 more minutes
  If rice starts to stick, add 2 tbs of water
- Eat the fried rice from small round bowls. Use chopsticks.
  See how to use chopsticks on (p 86)

What to say
- Chinese food is fried over a high heat in a big pan called a wok. Food is stirred all the time so that's why it's called stir-frying!
- The Chinese have cooked with woks for over 5,000 years
- Over a billion people live in China and most eat rice 3 times a day!
- This doesn't half keep the farmers busy in the paddy fields. They are usually able to grow two rice crops a year
- The Chinese cook rice in many different ways. This recipe is a great favourite for using up left-overs

Indonesian coconut chicken

What is it?
A recipe for coconut chicken. The coconut adds a delicious creamy flavour. Serve with plain boiled rice and it should stretch to 8 small servings.

What do you need?
- 4 chicken portions
- 3 tbs vegetable oil
- 2 onions, chopped
- 3 cloves of garlic, peeled and crushed
- 60g/2oz cream of coconut
- 300ml/1/2 pint hot water
- 1 tbs lemon juice
- 1 tsp ground ginger
- 1 tsp chilli powder
- pinch salt and pepper

What do you do?
- Heat the oil in a large frying pan
  Gently lower the chicken portions into it
  Cook for about 5 minutes on both sides
- Lift chicken portions on to kitchen paper
  Sprinkle with ginger, chilli powder, salt, pepper and lemon juice
- Fry the onions and garlic until soft
  Dissolve creamed coconut in hot water to make a thin, white milk
- Put chicken back into the pan and pour coconut milk over the top
  Cook over a low heat for about 40 minutes
- Serve on a plate with rice and enjoy the experience!

What to say
Indonesia is made up of over 13,000 islands. They are so famous for their spices that for centuries, people called them The Spice Islands. More coconuts grow in Indonesia than anywhere else in the world. Indonesian farmers can grow rice, sugar, peanuts and coconuts, as most of their land is good for farming. They send spices such as pepper, nutmeg, coriander and cloves all over the world.

Coconut milk shake

What is it?
A recipe for a delicious milk shake from the Philippines.

What do you need?
- 7 fl oz/200ml thin coconut milk (if coconut milk isn't available from the supermarket, check out your local health food shop)
- 4 tbsp sugar
- 2 sachets vanilla sugar or vanilla flavouring
- 7 fl oz thick coconut milk
- crushed ice
- a saucepan and wooden spoon
- tall glasses
- drinking straws

What do you do?
- Bring thin coconut milk to the boil
- Add sugar and vanilla. Stir until dissolved.
- Reduce heat and gently simmer for 10 minutes
- Leave to cool
- Add thick coconut milk and stir vigorously
- Add 6-8 tbsp crushed ice and beat thoroughly
- Pour the milk into tall glasses and drink with a straw

What to say?
Did you know that in Asia you don't get milk from cows? You get it from coconuts!

Coconut trees, unlike cows, are everywhere in East Asia! Local children can shin up a tree as quick as anything. They pick a ripe coconut, hack it open, and drink fresh coconut milk straight from the shell.

Fruit feast with coconut dip

What is it?
A recipe for an Asian dessert made from tropical fruits.

What do you need?
- A selection of tropical fruits, tinned or fresh: pineapples, melons, papayas, mangoes, tangerines, lychees, passion fruit, guavas
- 1 packet of chopped peanuts (check that all the children can eat these)
- 1 jug of semi-frozen lemonade (prepare this beforehand)
- 1 cup of coconut cream
- 1 serving plate
- 1 mixing bowl and 1 big spoon
- cocktail sticks
- spoons, knives and small cups (you may want to use plastic cutlery and cups)

What do you do?
- All help chop fruit into small chunks and arrange on a serving plate
- Sprinkle with peanuts
- Make the dip by mixing the lemonade and coconut cream
- Spoon individual portions of coconut cream into the cups
- Children pick up fruit chunks with cocktail sticks and tuck into the dip

What to say?
In Asia people don't usually eat sweet desserts, they enjoy feasting on tropical fruit. These are deliciously mouthwatering and very healthy!

Oodles of noodles

What is it?

A recipe for a quick and simple noodle soup that is a big favourite in Asia.

What do you need?

- Several packets of instant noodles (enough for children to each have a little dish)
- Bits of ham, corned beef, peas, corn, snow peas or bean sprouts (optional)
- One bowl and pair of chopsticks per child

What do you do?

- Bring water to boil in a large pan (see the noodle packet for measurements)
- Pop in the noodles with the flavour sachet. Follow instructions on the packet.
- Add some of the above ingredients for extra taste (or anything else you fancy)
- Serve in small bowls (one for each child)
- Grab your chopsticks and start munching!

Other ideas

- Make one or two thin omelettes ahead of time. Cut into strips. Sprinkle on top of the noodles once they are in each dish.

What to say?

Many people think noodles come from Italy, but Marco Polo brought them from China on his travels. For 2,000 years street stalls and wagons all over Asia have been selling bowls of boiled or fried noodles for fast food. They make a delicious snack. Do they beat McDonald's?! You decide!

Mango ice cream

What is it?

A recipe for a 2 litre tub of tropical ice cream.

What do you need?

- 1 sachet gelatine
- 1 tbsp lemon juice
- 1 large mango
- 180g sugar
- 375ml double cream
- 1 empty 2 litre plastic tub
- a hand blender

What do you do?

- Chop the mango into cubes
- Add sugar and lemon juice and mix together with the mango
- Make up the gelatine and mix it in
- Whip cream until nearly set
- Add to mango mixture and stir everything together
- Spoon mixture into tub
- Freeze until half set
- Blend the mixture and return to freezer
- Take the ice cream out 15 minutes before you want to serve it and enjoy!

What to say?

Mangoes are about the most delicious of all tropical fruits and this ice cream makes great party food. Why not keep the party atmosphere going with some ideas from the Games section. Start with 'Mango, mango, durian!' (p 82).

Resources

Contents

Maps of Asia

Maps of Asia

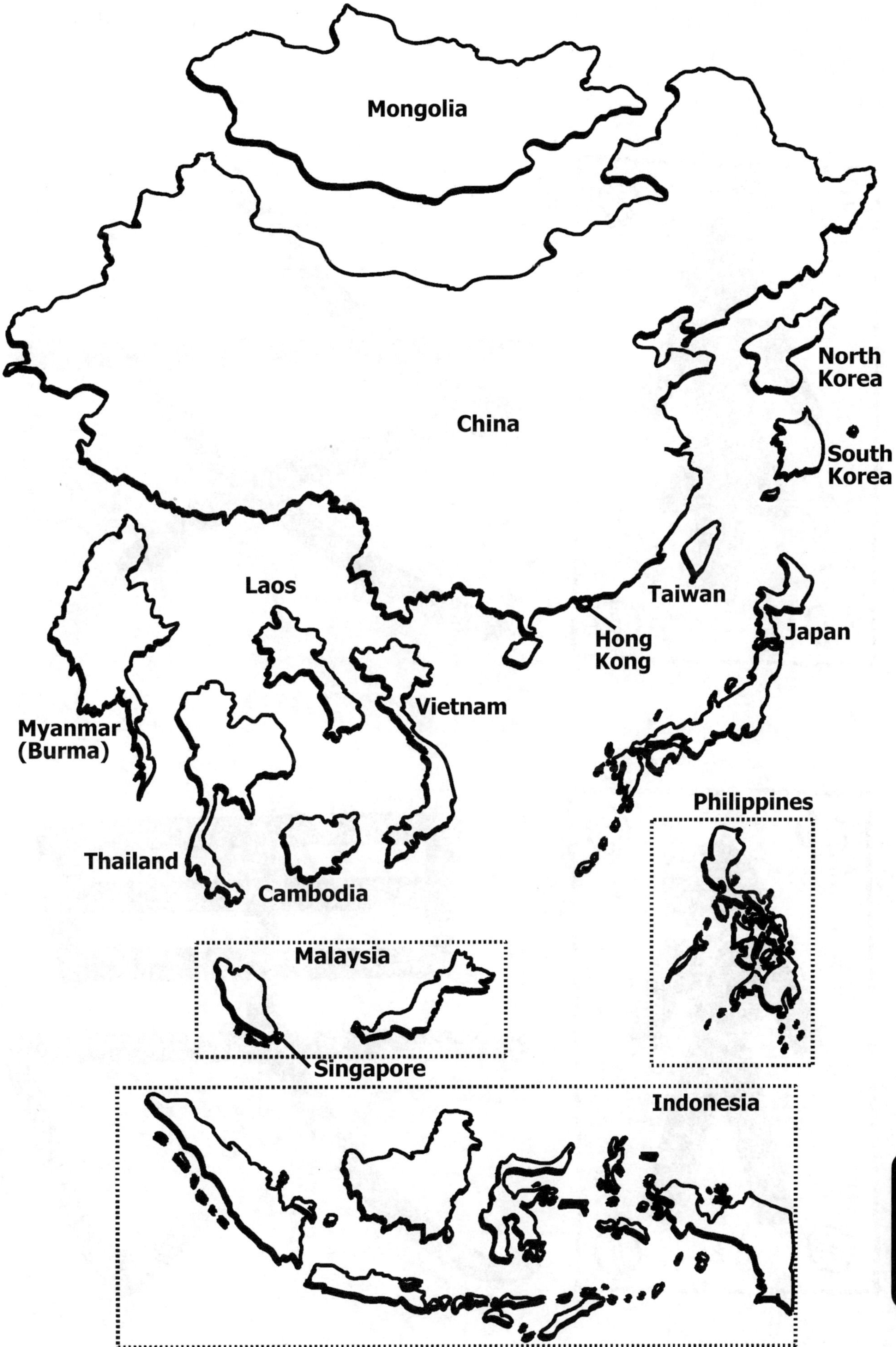
Mongolia
China
North Korea
South Korea
Taiwan
Hong Kong
Japan
Laos
Vietnam
Myanmar (Burma)
Thailand
Cambodia
Philippines
Malaysia
Singapore
Indonesia

Toilet signs

Use in game on p 79. Photocopy and enlarge them.

男 = male
女 = female

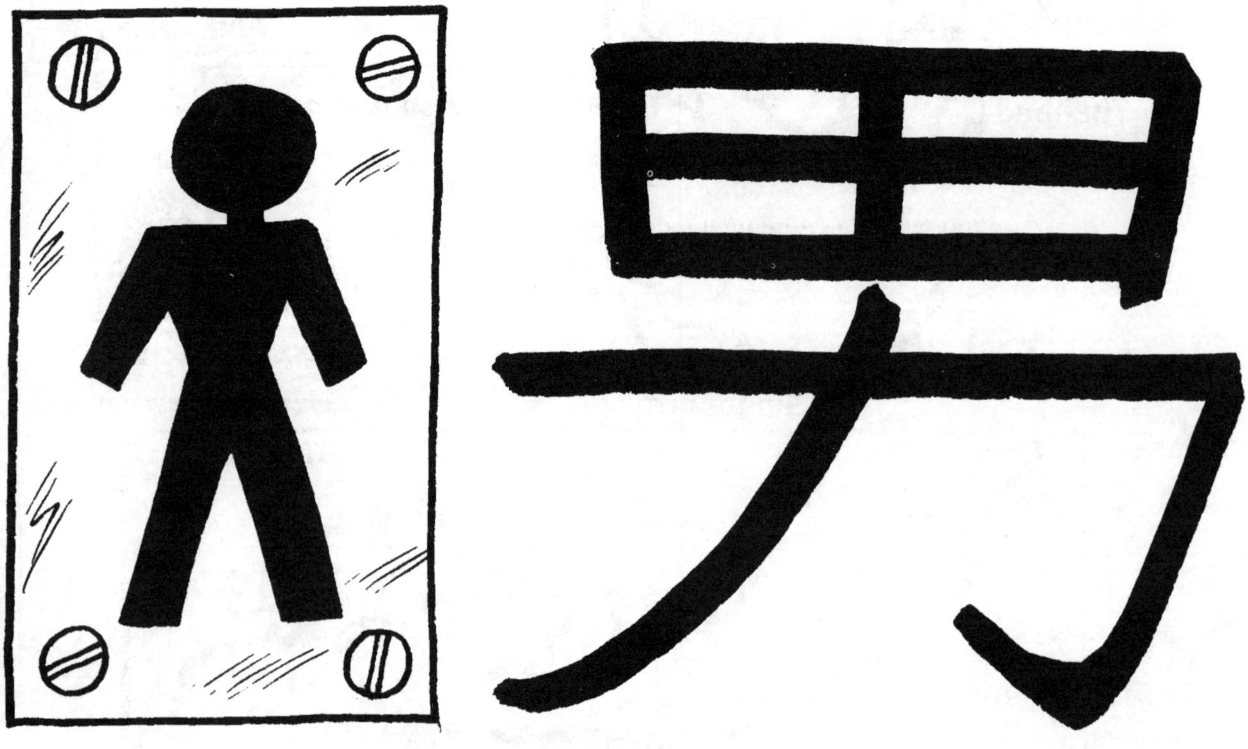

Where on earth...?

Country name

Number of people living here

Draw a map

Draw an animal from here

What is the main religion?
What do the people believe?

What is the weather like?

Interesting fact

Three things I should pray for

1

2

3

My name

Index by country

Most of the materials in this book are not tied to a particular country. You can use them to talk about mission anywhere in Asia or the rest of the world.

China

Indonesia

Japan

Philippines

Thailand

Asia general

Bible teaching

Resources